# SIGNS OF STRUGGLE

# SIGNS OF STRUGGLE

## The Rhetorical Politics of Cultural Difference

Thomas R. West

State University of New York Press

Published by
State University of New York Press, Albany

Printed in the United States of America

For information, address State University of New York Press, 90
State Street, Suite 700, Albany, NY, 12207

Production by Christine L. Hamel
Marketing by Michael Campochiaro

**Library of Congress Cataloging-in-Publication Data**

West, Thomas R., 1965–
    Signs of struggle : the rhetorical politics of cultural difference
    / by Thomas R. West.
        p. cm.
    Includes bibliographical references and index.
    ISBN 0791452972 (alk. paper)—ISBN 0791452980 (pbk.: alk. paper)
    1. Multiculturalism. 2. Ethnicity. 3. Pluralism (Social Sciences). I. Title.

HM1271.W47 2002                   2001042055
305.8—dc21                       CIP

The author gratefully acknowledges permission to reprint previously
published material. Parts of chapter 1 appeared in *JAC: A Journal of
Composition Theory* 19 (1999): 241–51 [with G. Olson] and in *The
Review of Education/Pedagogy/Cultural Studies* 21 (1999): 149–63
[with G.Olson]. (Reprinted by permission.) An earlier version of chapter 5 originally appeared as "The Rhetoric of Therapy and the Politics
of Anger: From the Safe House to a Praxis of Shelter" in *Rhetoric
Review* 19 (2000): 42–58. (Copyright 2000 by *Rhetoric Review*; reprinted by permission.)

*Dedicated to*

*Greta and Aidan*
*for making my life strangely and wonderfully different*

*and to Joanne, Bo, and Mike*
*for being there*

# Contents

# Foreword

## Toward a Productive Engagement
## with Cultural Difference

### Gary A. Olson

In April of 1992, Los Angeles was rocked by devastating riots after three police officers were acquitted of "assault under color of authority" for the brutal beating of Rodney King. The riots were responsible for fifty deaths, for nearly a billion dollars in property damage, and for focusing the national public attention on issues of race relations and cultural difference. It was in an attempt to quell these riots, to cool the heat of racial passions, that King himself addressed the nation and uttered the haunting question that will forever signify liberal anxiety: "Can't we all just get along?" In six short words, King had in effect managed to express an entire political philosophy that had begun as far back as seventeenth-century England, a philosophy impelled by bourgeois dread of conflict; white, middle-class fear of otherness (how ironic that these six words were uttered by a working-class black man); liberal insistence on papering over all cultural difference by insisting that "deep down" all humans are "the same," that our differences are only on the surface ("skin-deep," as they say) and thus are of little consequence. This liberal ideology of homogenization has been a part of American political philosophy since the inception of the United States as an independent nation, and it is perhaps represented most aptly in the metaphor of "the melting pot." This image of homogenization, of the blending of all difference into one single mass, is so burned into the consciousness of all citizens that it hardly seems conceivable to question whether a "melting pot" really is a desirable approach to constructing a multicultural society, whether erasing cultural difference benefits all citizens or just those in dominant positions; whether what "melts" away are really all the ethnic and racial traits that mark certain people as *not* white, *not* Western European, *not* Christian, and so on. So ingrained in the national imaginary is this understanding of what a "true" democracy is, that to many it hardly seems worthwhile to train a critical lens on it.

Of course, this failure to deal productively and not reductively with difference has been the subject of sustained critique in recent years from a variety of critical discourses, including feminist theory, postcolonial theory, queer studies, critical race studies, and critical legal studies. But, as is so often the case, rhetoric and composition has been dreadfully slow in responding to intellectual developments occurring outside its own borders. Finally, however, scholars within the field are beginning to draw on these critiques and to theorize rhetoric's role in thinking a productive politics of difference. Thomas West's *Signs of Struggle* serves as a major breakthrough in this effort. Sophisticated, intelligent, and engaging, *Signs of Struggle* attempts to move beyond a liberal pluralist approach to difference, one that merely acknowledges or "celebrates" diversity, toward a productive *engagement* with difference. West examines how liberal pluralism serves to allay national anxiety over cultural difference by reassuring a white, bourgeois populace through an assortment of rhetorical and political processes, including the commodification, fetishization, and exoticization of difference. He argues cogently that intellectuals in rhetoric and composition have an obligation, both in our scholarship and in our classrooms, to critique and resist simplistic media-produced versions of cultural identity.

Proposing a guideline for understanding community as an assemblage of what he calls "compositions of difference," West theorizes a rhetorical politics and a political rhetoric that engages cultural differences on their own terms, without glossing over the very real tensions and conflicts inherent in them. Thus, this is an eminently hopeful, optimistic book, in that West suggests that there are indeed ways to "recompose" communities within difference and dissimilarity, ways to recompose the rhetorical-political conditions in such a way that difference is allowed to flourish, thereby enriching rather than impoverishing community. Clearly, this is a thorough repudiation of melting-pot ideology and a radical recognition of the creative potential of cultural difference.

Drawing on a diverse assortment of scholars in rhetoric and composition—from Linda Brodkey to Robert Connors to Lynn Worsham—and on an equally diverse group from other fields—including Gloria Anzaldúa, Homi Bhabha, and Henry Giroux—West deftly explores how rhetoric and composition can engage with other discourses to devise a "rhetorical politics" of difference that escapes the theoretical and political impasses of previous work. This is a smart, incisive, and constructive examination of how rhetoric, composition, culture, and politics intersect in important, sometimes troubling, always significant ways. Simply put, *Signs of Struggle* represents composition theory at its finest. For anyone committed to the role of rhetoric in the struggle for social justice, *Signs of Struggle* is a must-read.

*University of South Florida*
*Tampa, Florida*

# Acknowledgments

Many people have helped in the writing and production of this book. My sincerest thanks go to Gary Olson for his close reading of earlier drafts of this manuscript, and especially for his encouragement and generosity throughout our working together. I also want to thank Priscilla Ross for all her efforts in finding the book a home; the folks at SUNY Press, especially Christine Hamel; Pete Vandenberg for his contribution; and thanks go to Bruce Horner for that heroic work writers seek and value so much: in-depth feedback, discerning insight, crucial comments and suggestions.

Thanks especially to Garet Cox for her understanding and for graciously giving her time and energy so that I could complete this project. I also want to acknowledge the personal and professional camaraderie of fellow (and future) graduates of the rhetoric and composition program at the University of South Florida. Thanks to my friends Walter Lewallen and Jerry Lucas for their complicitous and critical interest in science fiction—and other things pop culture, avant-garde, and generally geekish. And thanks finally to Larry Beason, Bob Coleman, Michelle Comstock, Sue Walker, and Jim White for their friendship and for their interest in and support of writing at the University of South Alabama.

# Introduction

# Compositions of Difference

> Certainly there are very real differences between us of
> race, age, and sex. But it is not those differences between
> us that are separating us. It is rather our refusal to
> recognize those differences, and to examine the distor-
> tions that result from our misnaming them and their
> effects upon human behavior and expectation.
>
> —Audre Lorde

Critically considering the ways in which cultural differences are
regarded and represented remains a crucial part of the study of rhetoric
and culture, especially in times of rapid and intense social transformation.
This is because cultural differences are not things that exist independent
of social contexts and power relations; they are, rather, *signs of struggle*,
interpretations of human tendencies, practices, features, and customs
defined in the relationships and struggles among groups of people in
particular contexts for particular reasons. In this sense, cultural differences are supremely rhetorical: they are defined in language and have real
consequences. They are about the ways in which groups of people feel,
talk, and think about other groups of people; about the assumptions and
judgments groups make about other groups; about how those assumptions
and judgments "compose" society—how they influence philosophy,
determine policy, and incite action. Too many times, however, differences are represented superficially and indifferently, we might say, in
ways that merely acknowledge and celebrate them—or, worse, in ways

1

that outright objectify and commodify them. For example, on television ads we constantly see women and men of all ages and cultures playing, trading, working, and computing in an endless proliferation of consumer desires. In the heart of Florida, Disney's Epcot Center serves as an eerie analogue to the idea of a harmonious pluralism; here countries and cultures exist safely side-by-side, partitioned, exoticized, and commodified, sanitized and neatly packaged for perusal. Even the ostensibly progressive *Star Trek* shows, for example, continue to play out allegories of liberal pluralism, projecting a pluralist future which ensures us, with all the didacticism of traditional allegory, that all we need in the face of difficult times is unflagging dedication to righteous liberal-democratic principles. In contexts of benign pluralism and boutique multiculturalism—in which difference is increasingly commodified, managed, and co-opted—the central issue is not "one of merely *acknowledging* difference; rather, the more difficult question concerns the kind of difference that is acknowledged and engaged. Difference seen as benign variation (diversity), for instance, rather than as conflict, struggle, or the threat of disruption, bypasses power as well as history to suggest a harmonious, empty pluralism" (Mohanty 146). Co-option and commodification are ways of handling differences, of managing them in ways that serve to reassure a population increasingly anxious about the uncertainties of cultural differences. In these times of dizzying global expansion, it is increasingly important for critical rhetorical and cultural theory to continue to trace the rhetorical and political processes of cultural differentiation, to take stands against commodifying, fetishizing, and exoticizing differences, and to recognize just how representations of differences are connected to particular agendas.

But while we have innocuous versions of liberal pluralism that often seek to gloss over real tensions and conflict, we also have the kinds of hate politics that represent otherness as unintelligible, unreasonable, threatening, and/or evil—a politics characterized by scapegoating, isolationism, obsession, and cruelty. To most of us, demonizing differences is more than noxious: such responses not only devalue and denigrate that which is different, but they often involve processes of dehumanization that can lead to violent extremism. Most of us would agree that it is crucial to work against processes of cultural differentiation that demonize differences. But, more than this, if we are to learn from our differences rather than simply tolerate them, if we are to learn how to create livable, viable, and various futures, it is important to critique and resist the easy-going, multicultural, media-packaged versions of cultural identity as well.

Audre Lorde's point on this matter is well-taken: "Difference must be not merely tolerated, but seen as a fund of necessary polarities between which our creativity can spark like dialectic" (111). The problem with tolerance is that such an approach does not go far enough toward creating varied social space based on irreducible differences; it seeks merely to endure or bear differences (for how long?), thereby discouraging the kind "dialectic spark" necessary for co-constituted social relations and real, ongoing change. But doing more than merely tolerating differences raises important questions not easily answered: What kinds of rhetorical politics should be advanced in order to encourage differences to be more than merely expressed, tolerated, and celebrated? How can we accept the risk of disruption to the status quo that irreducible difference may represent—what we might call the transformative potential of the otherness of the other—without resorting to an "anything goes" style of rhetorical politics? How can we foster social relations dependent on states of knowledge that are prepared to suffer modification and interrogation by what they neither possess nor can claim as their own? (Chambers 50). These are the guiding problems I would like to keep in front of us throughout this book as I critique the kinds of cultural-rhetorical politics—both liberal and neo-conservative—that disallow for enabling, engaging, and accepting differences on their own terms.

In this book I want to articulate a rhetorical politics that fosters the critical gravity of difference, accepting and engaging differences on their own terms, and posit a guideline for viewing community as an assemblage of "compositions of difference." Let me explain what I mean by "compositions of difference" by using an American Movie Corporation advertisement. The ad depicts a "person" made of strips of film preparing to conduct an imaginary orchestra. The title of the composition on the conductor's music stand is "There is a Difference," AMC's slogan. But when the conductor taps the rack with his baton for attention, the entire composition collapses in a cascade of notes. The ad ends, and the composition, it seems, we are never to hear. AMC's slogan, "There is a difference," however, remains, and it offers an illustrative meditation on processes of cultural differentiation. AMC wants viewers to know that their theaters are different from others, that there is a difference in movie-going experiences, that some theaters are better than others. The company would not highlight such a difference if they offered what they thought were inferior facilities—or maybe they would! Their point, though, is that "there is a difference," and AMC's theaters are better for whatever reasons—more comfortable seating, better sound quality, friendlier service. A company claiming that its goods and services are different and, thus, better than those of their competitors is nothing new. Likewise, groups of people highlighting that "there is a difference" between themselves and others is nothing new either. In fact, throughout history people have defined, and continue to define, one another by their differences. But differences in skin color or physical features, for example, are not the problems; rather, the problem is the negative characteristics and qualities ascribed to the other on the basis of these differences. It is through "ideologies of difference" that people come to be marked negatively—not white, not European, not male, for example—in order to relegate their rights to an inferior or lesser status (Said 41). What is important to realize is that these differences have played formative historic roles in the ranking of human subjectivities, significant ways that groups have posited themselves as "better"—more advanced, more civilized, more reasonable, and so on—than other groups. This is how difference in relation to group identity formation works, and such a strategy of cultural differentiation is part of "the rhetorical politics of cultural difference."

If differences are "composed," or inscribed into culture, then they can be recomposed so as to operate less monologically and monoculturally. The idea of "compositions of difference" suggests that there are ways of "composing"—or, more accurately, "recomposing"—communities grounded in dissimilarity and difference, not always in consensus and conformity. I hope this idea might act as a theoretical guideline for resisting the kinds of politics of difference mentioned above (those of uncritical multiculturalism and those of hate) and act as a heuristic for (re)composing the rhetorical-political conditions in which differences are allowed to flourish creatively, critically, and variously. Edward Said, for example, says, "One can declare oneself *for* difference (as opposed to sameness or homogenization) without at the same time being for the rigidly enforced and policed separation of populations into different groups" (40). In other words, one can declare oneself for the right to be different, and argue for a conception of the *civitas* based on difference and dissensus, not necessarily on conformity and uniformity, without viewing groups as discrete social items that cannot make claims beyond their own borders. Social categorization is not monologically determined, although it sometimes appears so; that is, people can work to change the perhaps rigid and narrow definitions of social categories by drawing on their "categorical" or group and individual experiences as well as by working from principled, theoretical stances. What I want to articulate is a critical agenda that involves expanding the ground rules for risky interaction, while it recognizes, analyzes, and critiques the rhetorical politics of othering at every turn. "Compositions of difference" are forms of community that more than tolerate disruptive difference (that which one cannot claim as one's own); they are forms of community that, consequently, must creatively and forcefully rearticulate the ground rules for hegemonic struggle, ideological conflict, and contested versions of citizenship.

Expanding multiculturalist causes and furthering ways to recompose difference necessarily includes research into and arguments for interaction based not on conformity and uniformity but on dissimilarity and difference. To do more than express, tolerate, and celebrate cultural differences means, among other things, to critique the leveling effect of uncritical pluralism that suggests that all groups "have a relative equality of articulation within the space of American intellectual culture" (Dyson 153). It is to inquire into how differences have been and continue to be written or inscribed into the cultural imaginary, and how this in turn affects social and educational policy as well as how people think and feel about one another. The versions of multiculturalism I advance seek to create forums for bringing various viewpoints into dialogue with one another in order to alter understanding and facilitate change, highlighting and exploiting rather than suppressing and ignoring the co-constitutive and multi-determinant dimensions of engagement and interaction. Realizing that terms and identities are not natural or given but struggled for in social contexts allows for a rhetorical strategy that Teresa Ebert calls "rewriting." Ebert explains this as

> "activating" the "other" suppressed and concealed by dominant modes of knowing [and articulating] the unsaid, the suppressed, not only of texts and signifying practices but also of the theories and frames of intelligibilities shaping them. Voicing this silenced "other" displaces the dominant logic—dislodging its hegemony and demystifying its "naturalness"—and unleashes alternative potential. (888)

What is needed in the face of those politics that restrict the "right" to be different are strategies for "rewriting" social and pedagogical relations around conditions that foster not merely a celebration of diversity but an agonistic or tense plurality. We might think of such a tense plurality as the play of various critical methods and traditions in order to generate multi-determinant forms of knowledge about cultural differences. Articulating such critical projects necessarily means critiquing some of the more cherished ideals of liberalism: tolerance, civility, and governance through negotiated consensus. This is not to say that these ideals are bankrupt but rather that they are sources of conflict (although typically not seen as such) over what comes to count as legitimate interaction and acceptable inclusion in "democratic" and "civil" societies. Critiques of the rhetorical politics of othering must also include study of the affective dimensions of difference, the role of what Peter Lyman has referred to as "the paralanguages of emotion" in the politics of difference. Because racism and sexism are in part affectively motivated and psychically inscribed in our minds and bodies, they cannot be effectively countered by mapping new ways of thinking onto old ways of feeling, highlighting the need to be critical of the highly emotionally charged rhetorical politics of difference (Worsham, "Going" 216).

For the last quarter of the twentieth century, questions of cultural difference have been posed largely through discourses of multiculturalism, discourses that typically posit a multicultural society in terms of diversity and pluralism, a society of various diverse yet distinct groups—sometimes called races or cultures—interacting and living among one another. Multiculturalism certainly has had its proponents and detractors. There are those neoconservative positions that oppose multiculturalism on the grounds that it erodes a shared, common culture, that it represents a "PC" pandering to whatever culture or group cries foul. Multiculturalism, however, has its proponents on the left. Growing out of the civil rights movement, multiculturalism clearly has been helpful in increasing awareness of and respect for the needs and interests of historically disenfranchised groups. Yet, critical thinkers have convincingly argued that the code words associated with multiculturalism and liberalism—civility, diversity, pluralism, tolerance—have more to do with universally imposing the monocultural and monological ideals of liberalism to heterogeneous situations and less to do with enabling and engaging differences on their own terms. That is, the "rightness" of these key concepts of liberalism and liberal-democratic procedures is often above question, reinforcing faith in their impartiality and helping to rationalize their uncritical imposition in all matters of difference. As Stanley Fish puts it, "The liberal strategy is to devise (or attempt to devise) procedural mechanisms that are neutral with respect to point of view and therefore can serve to frame partisan debates in a nonpartisan manner" (16). Of late, radical theorists have initiated sustained and formidable critiques of multiculturalism and its attendant logic of liberal impartiality. Henry

Giroux and the Chicago Cultural Studies Group, for example, have forwarded strains of multiculturalism that are insurgent and critical. These moves are meant to nuance our understandings of multiculturalism and challenge forms that merely acknowledge the existence of difference. Critical forms of multiculturalism seek to hold multiculturalism to its promise "to make political culture open and responsible, not only to diverse viewpoints, but also to the conflicts that liberal procedures normally screen out" (Berlant and Warner 107). Furthermore, some scholars argue that versions of multiculturalism that are merely celebratory and non-critical can actually squelch rather than promote difference by eliding, distorting, or at least obfuscating "the incredible heterogeneity and raucous diversity that is contained in any minority identity" (Dyson 153).[1]

Because some of the more urgent guiding problems facing scholars of rhetoric and culture continue to center on teaching, discussing, and representing cultural differences in ways that do not avoid issues of social, political, and material inequality, it is increasingly important to approach cultural difference as not a "natural emanation of the fact that there are different cultures in the world," as postcolonial theorist Homi Bhabha says, but as a "particular constructed discourse at a time when something is being challenged about power and authority." When something is being challenged about power and authority, he continues,

> a particular cultural trait or tradition—the smell of somebody's food, the color of their skin, the accent that they speak with, their particular history, be it Irish or Indian or Jewish—becomes the site of contestation, abuse, insult, and discrimination. Cultural difference is not a natural emanation of the fact that there are different cultures in the world. It's a much more problematic and sophisticated reproduction of a ritual, a habit, a trait, a characteristic. The reproduction has to bear a whole set of significations, tensions, anxieties. And it becomes the sign of those tensions and anxieties. Cultural difference is not difficult, if you like, because there are many diverse cultures; it is because there is some particular issue about the redistribution of goods between cultures, or the funding of cultures, or the emergence of minorities or immigrants in a situation of resources—where resource allocation has to go—or the construction of schools and the decision about whether the school should be bilingual or trilingual or whatever. It is at that point that the problem of cultural difference is produced. So, it's really an argument against the naturalization of the notion of culture. ("Staging" 16)

What Bhabha refers to as "cultural *difference*" is not the same thing as "cultural *diversity*." Cultural diversity is a way of thinking about difference on which much multicultural thinking rests: that there are diverse yet distinct and essential categories of people. Questions of the historical constitution of difference are not issues to be taken up but rather ones to be avoided in attempts at accommodation. The historical constitution of difference, genealogies of difference, is elided while a policy of accommodation is forwarded, a policy that recognizes, respects, and celebrates difference *as diversity* but one that typically does not inquire into difference *as alterity*, as the politics of "othering" people for particular reasons. On the other hand, a concept of cultural *difference*, according to Bhabha, highlights the need to interrogate precisely how differences have been defined and (mis)represented in order to influence and determine the circulation of representations, rights, and goods.

The study of engagement, consequently, is important to the rhetorical politics of cultural difference, and, for this reason, I examine the rhetorical strategy of negotiation in Chapter 1 and identify important links between writing and the concept of cultural hybridity as a form of identity negotiation. I bring critical pressure to bear on traditional notions of negotiation as compromise, the art of the deal, and forward guidelines for *critical negotiation*, a way of thinking about negotiation less as a mere dealing and more as a postcolonial dialogic process or ethics of engagement. Also, working from insights of Bhabha and "borderland" writer Gloria Anzaldúa, I argue for hybridity, a kind of negotiation of cultural codes, to be understood as a rhetorical and discursive strategy of resistance to notions of social identity restricted and fixed by racial thinking. This chapter further lays the theoretical groundwork on critical negotiation for the next two chapters.

In Chapter 2, I contend that analyzing race as a discourse of difference that situates groups of people hierarchically is crucial to furthering multiculturalist causes. Much multicultural rhetoric emphasizes accommodating diversity rather than examining how differences have been historically constituted, thereby often preserving ingrained beliefs and practices concerning cultural difference. It is not enough that we merely celebrate our differences; it is important to research the historical constitution of cultural difference not only to work to dismantle the debilitating effects of racism in the present but to understand better the connections between race, writing, and learning. This must include, I argue, critical investigations into the cultural signification of whiteness.

Chapter 3 examines how critical men's studies interrogates constructions of hegemonic masculinity, not in order to hold up masculinity as a privileged object of study, as is sometimes thought, but to examine how hegemonic forms of masculinity are in part socially constructed as oppressive and exploitative and how they may be reconstructed along less oppressive and less restrictive lines. I argue that part of the project of countering gender discrimination must be enacted by men who are willing, despite the "objective inadequacy" of *male feminism*, to counter it in open and honest ways. This chapter is in part a response to Robert J. Connors' *College English* article, "Teaching and Learning as a Man."

In Chapter 4, I research how today's politics of difference work on a deep affective level; I explore the fact that how people *feel* about one another is intimately connected to how they *act* toward one another. Critical theory and critical pedagogy have typically overlooked and under-engaged the role of affect and emotion in social and political engagement. Too often emotions are dismissed as unimportant and non-political. This is not because emotions are inherently non-political but because they have been relegated largely to the realm of the individual and the psychological. As some feminist theorists have argued, it is important to understand emotion more explicitly in political and social terms, that we are motivated to act politically and socially not by reason alone but by passion and feeling. Sandra Lee Bartky has argued also for critical examination of the role of emotions, especially those of assessment, in the perpetuation of subjection. To study the affective politics and relations of difference, it is important to expand rhetorical analysis to include examining the politics of emotion as well as the emotion of politics.

Although there has been much discussion in rhetorical theory about the importance of "contact zones," conflict, and dissensus to the process of learning, there has been less talk of the relationship between "safe houses" (and shelter in general) and conflict. In Chapter 5, I argue that if we are to advance agonistic pedagogical models, then it is also important to theorize shelter and the psychic fallout of engagement in relation to matters of cultural difference. What is needed in this case is a reexamination of therapeutic rhetoric in pedagogical discourse. By individualizing the effects of alienation, exploitation, and oppression, much rhetoric of therapy discourages public, collective forms of protest against the broader conditions of human alienation, exploitation, and oppression that are social and political in nature. To supplement traditional understandings of therapy, I articulate *a praxis of shelter*, a position on shelter that seeks to politicize individual and psychological "problems" by attempting to understand the suffering and healing of individuals and groups explicitly in terms of social, political, and economic conditions. Chapters 4 and 5 cohere around issues of emotion and difference.

In my conclusion, I sketch directions for further study of the ways in which rhetorical positions and forms of argumentation get "othered"— how they are dismissed as too outside or extreme by conventions of community or propriety or civility. Positing more agonistic or radical forms of interaction than is possible in liberalism's schema of negotiated consensus, I argue for the importance of expanding the ground rules for rhetorical and political engagement and for working toward forums that are more inclusive and understanding of irreducible differences. I also argue for a renewed understanding of *culture*, and "cultures," as consti- tuted *in difference, as difference* in order to articulate a hermeneutics of cultural rhetoric that takes into account processes of cultural differentia- tion as involving the anxieties of groups concerning their relationships to other groups.

Linda Brodkey has argued for the need to recognize that "the negative valuing of difference—*not* white, *not* male, *not* heterosexual, *not* middle class—is socially constructed and can therefore be socially reconstructed and positively revalued" (159). "Transvaluing difference," according to her, is a reconstructive theoretical and pedagogical project that traces and critiques the negative discriminatory effects of differencing others reductively ("not white," "not male," for example). It further seeks to revalue differences positively and in more complex ways by facilitating processes wherein differences are valued across and against one another (transvalued) and not unilaterally imposed. For Brodkey, it is important to see difference

> not as an attribute of someone or something, but as a negative quality that is *imputed* to someone or something as an essential and defining feature that rationalizes the surveillance and regulation of an entire population in search of the often trivial but consequential "differences" that justify systematically isolating groups of people for special and inequitable treatment. It is not difference but systematic denials of these regimes of surveillance and regulation that divide us. It is these regimes that authorize the commonsense epistemologies that consistently represent difference as negation or lack or abnormality that most students know. It is these versions that those who insist on redefining their differences in positive

rather than negative terms seek to subvert. And it is varieties of commonsense epistemology that pedagogy must transvalue, for if multiculturalism is to be seen as a part of the regeneration of a society rather than held up as the fetish of its decline, difference must be posed as a condition of community. (195)

The concept of *difference*, of course, has been used in poststructural critical discourse for some time in order to challenge notions that the meanings of words naturally correspond to the things and ideas they describe and that social identities are given or natural. Such a concept of difference has become one of the more evocative ways of thinking about how meanings and identities are constituted *in relation to* other meanings and other identities and how these relations involve questions of power. That is, the meanings of words and of the social identities they "describe" result in large part from the struggle among people to define words and identities in cultural and political forums: "What these signs mean is not given or natural, but rather the outcome of struggles over the signifiers and meanings used to make sense of them. The relation between word and world, language and social reality or, in short, 'difference,' is not the result of textuality but the effect of social struggle" (Ebert 887). Viewing identity and meaning as constructed relationally and in struggle rather than as simply given is of enormous import to scholars of culture and rhetoric who are interested in interrogating the negative, discriminatory rhetorics of racism and sexism, as well as those seeking powerful heuristics for rhetorical and cultural analyses of social inequality. Perhaps most importantly, viewing identity and meaning as constructed relationally allows for struggle against monological and monocultural determinism. Rigorous analysis and strategic redeployment of *difference* are key to critical projects in cultural and rhetorical studies that seek to challenge received wisdom that claims that any group—identified by race, gender, class, or sexual orientation—is naturally and, thus, permanently socially situated. It is not our differences themselves that divide us, as Brodkey says, but denial of the discriminatory effects of the differences that matter—those of social, political, and economic inequality.

While the buzzwords of multiculturalism—diversity and pluralism—account for the existence of different populations, neither of them registers the fact that difference is, as Joan Scott puts it, not simply a state of being, but a relationship: "There are no differences without comparisons, and these are usually made hierarchically in reference to something that has been established as the norm" (216). In order to have communities, or "compositions," of difference, Scott thinks there are certain points that must be addressed:

- Differences are often irreducible and must be accepted as such.

- Differences are relational, and involve hierarchy and differentials of power that are constantly contested.

- Conflict and contest are inherent in communities of difference. There must be ground rules for coexistence that do not presume the resolution of conflict and the discovery of consensus.

- Communities cannot be based on conformity, but on an acceptance and acknowledgment of difference. (223)

Seeing differences as often irreducible and non-negotiable, as sites and signs of struggle, is not to romanticize conflict and struggle; rather, it is to call into question the very logic of the reducibility of differences and the very terms of the politics of negotiated consensus. It is to realize that processes of cultural differentiation have always involved wrangles over real stakes that affect people's lives and the power to constitute reality. It is to realize that ignoring the often messy dimensions of difference represents, among other things, a kind of historical amnesia, a way of thinking about cultures as discrete and pristine social items that live "unsullied by the intertextuality of their historical locations" (Bhabha, *Location* 34)—much like the national exhibition-attractions at Epcot Center that I mentioned earlier. Seeing differences as sites and signs of struggle, as sources of conflict, also encourages multivalent forms of knowledge about "self" and "other." Dealing with difference is not always a neat and contained affair, and accepting differences on their own terms, so to speak, is also to accept the risk of difficulty, critique, disruption, change. For these reasons, it is important in positing communities and compositions of difference to articulate a hermeneutic of cultural rhetoric and ideological engagement that involves the critical study of processes of cultural differentiation as well as the interlocking dimensions of social experience. Such studies, I hope, can help us to learn and to teach theoretically grounded and socially responsible versions of difference while we work to compose communities of difference that do not collapse under the pressure of tension, communities that are not monologic, fragile, and rigid but multivalent, responsive, and open to revision.

# Chapter One

# Toward a Critical Theory of
# Negotiation and Hybridity

> To inhabit the multiplicity of cultural borders, historical temporalities, and hybrid identities calls for a state of knowledge, an ethics of the intellect, an aperture in politics, able to acknowledge more than itself; a state of knowledge that is prepared to suffer modification and interrogation by what it neither possesses nor can claim as its own.
>
> —Iain Chambers

> The question of hybridity is precisely to draw attention to the way in which the process of negotiation is continually placing and replacing the members of that act of cultural or social or political interaction.... We are always in the middle of difference.
>
> —Homi Bhabha

Perhaps no term in recent critical discourse has signaled the anxieties of difference, as well as liberal-democratic impulses for accommodation, more than "negotiation." Increasingly, scholars in cultural studies and rhetorical theory are using "negotiation" as a guiding metaphor for how people might work through and live with their differences. "Negotiation" has become a buzzword, and we hear regularly of the possibility of negotiating all kinds of things: conflicts, identities, meanings, borders—even our very differences. In fact, there is much optimism lately about the

13

possibility of negotiating our differences. Certainly, most of us want to be optimistic about living with and communicating our differences. After all, the objective of focusing on difference, at least to many postmodern thinkers, is to argue for the right to be different, to argue for a conception of the *civitas* based on difference and dissensus, not necessarily on conformity and uniformity. As some have argued, negotiation as a rhetorical strategy can help us to rethink the connections between the public sphere and students' writing, and negotiation can be a productive way to think of classroom interaction. Nonetheless, because negotiation also can act, and has acted, as a strategy of colonization disguised as civil interaction, and because we don't hear much critical discussion about what negotiation means to those who use this term, it poses particular problems as a guiding metaphor for social and political interaction. Furthermore, in order to achieve a critical perspective on negotiation, it is important to view recent language of negotiation in the context of increasingly insistent calls for civility, propriety, and politeness in political rhetoric and public life in general. For these reasons, it would serve us well to bring some critical pressure to bear on the concept of negotiation as it has been traditionally conceived and theorized, especially regarding matters of cultural difference.

A principal problem with how negotiation is used is that it most often refers to some utopian Rortian "conversation" that is supposed to lead, in some genteel fashion, to consensus, to an accommodation. It has become a code word for liberal aversion to conflict. Such an understanding of negotiation, however, is a sure prescription for depoliticizing the political, for continuing to prevent those without power from participating productively in political discourse. Slavoj Žižek argues that negotiation is a form of "parapolitics" and as such helps to *de*politicize politics. He describes parapolitics as the attempt "to deantagonize politics by way of formulating clear rules to be obeyed so that the agonistic procedure of litigation does not explode into politics proper" ("Leftist" 992). Negotiation as a form of parapolitics in effect disavows the logic of political antagonism. For political philosopher Chantal Mouffe, the move to make civil discourse "civil," to prevent people from engaging in the agonistic, adversarial, hegemonic struggle that *is* civil discourse, is a way to maintain the status quo because attempting to make such discourse "polite" serves only those already in positions of power in that it discourages the disenfranchised from attempting to take on subject positions, to represent their positions and interests forcefully. Thus, uncritically advancing and relying on negotiation both as a guiding metaphor and as a rhetorical strategy for engagement and interaction may result in a *de*politicizing of the ways in which we think of difference.

Another problem with negotiation is that it is usually understood in a strictly functional or instrumentalist sense, and such an understanding of interaction often does not take into account the role and effect of emotion and affect during negotiation. That is, dealing with difference in the real world is not neat, contained, and rational; it is often messy, sprawling, and emotional. In fact, Mouffe claims that one of the most powerful political forces is "passion": "That is what moves people to act in politics. It's not that reason and interests have no place, but I think that these are not the main motives for people to act. It's what I call 'passion.' Outrage, anger, empathy, sympathy, and those kinds of emotions are part of the same family in criticizing the rationalist model" ("Rethinking" 195). And Homi Bhabha adds that "the structures of feelings and the structures of affect are radically devalued in the language of political effectivity, cultural identity, and so on" ("Staging" 34).

Perhaps most importantly, there is not much historicizing of the concept of negotiation itself in cultural and rhetorical theory. If we think of negotiation as a way to work with our differences without at the same time being critical of the very concept of negotiation, we risk negotiation's becoming a cliché in the critical discourse, a floating signifier devoid of any truly descriptive power and open to anyone and everyone's private, dehistoricized spin on its definition and role. In short, if we are not critical of such liberal notions of negotiation, we risk incorporating them without reflection into our discussions of difference.

Despite the indifferent liberal conception of negotiation that seems to be so ubiquitous, as a rhetorical strategy and as a guiding metaphor negotiation still holds promise for accomplishing more than merely "expressing" differences. What is clearly needed is a theory of what might be called "critical negotiation," an understanding of negotiation that more consciously evokes its Latin roots: *to create a sense of unease.* That is, if we are to theorize negotiation as a strategy to enable us to work with our differences, then understanding negotiation as strict compromise or as navigation, as the smoothing over of tensions rather than the exploration and interrogation of them, needs to be supplemented and/or replaced by a model of critical negotiation, a strategy that highlights not only the (re)formation of meaning and subjectivity during moments of social and political interaction but one that also takes into account the role and effect of emotion during these moments. Negotiation should be conceived as a "borderland" rhetorical strategy connected to the ambivalent state of hybridity wherein the co-constitutive dimensions of identity and meaning formation are recognized and exploited by the disenfranchised; this is what Bhabha refers to as the "double-dealing" aspect of negotiation. We might think of critical negotiation as a strategy of "border pedagogy," as a strategy of "transgression in which existing borders forged in domination can be challenged and redefined" (Giroux 28). In this way, we can come to see negotiation not as merely the trading of pregiven objects or positions but as a moment of self- and co-definition that may be turned to advantage. Thus redefined, negotiation is associated with postcolonial critical strategies of "translation," "ambivalence," "resistance," and "hybridization."

## Hybridity as (Critical) Negotiation:
### The Translation of Identity

In order to understand negotiation as something other than navigation or compromise, it might be useful to recognize how hybridity may be deliberately deployed as a critical strategy to defy the monological and reductionist ways that race—one kind of difference—has traditionally defined people. Without ignoring the historical trajectories of race, postcolonial theorists such as Bhabha and "borderland" writers such as Gloria Anzaldúa have argued for deploying hybridity as a deliberate strategy to upset perilously settled social identities. Because there is continual temptation to think of racial identities as static and congealed, there is often little incentive to think of hybrid identities in positive terms. This is not because a hybrid state is somehow inherently flawed but because all too often the concept of race is seen as describing natural, distinct, and separate categories of people. That is, the hybrid state is often seen as flawed because it is not pure or pristine, because one "race" is diluting another. This, of course, is the old racist fear of miscegenation or race-mixing, "contaminating" a superior race with an inferior one. And this is why the hybrid has been posited as not "natural," as an affront to nature—particularly in times of social and political struggle over resources and the means to self-determination. Thinking of the hybrid as a "freak of nature" is a direct result of racial/racist thinking that posits natural, distinct, separate, and hierarchically arranged categories of people. Not only does such thinking discourage conceiving of hybrid identities in positive terms, it also discourages understanding how hybrid identities are the direct and indirect result of all manner of social transformations: displacement, immigration, occupation, relocation, migration, diaspora, slavery, etc.

More to the point, however, is that there is simply no such thing as a pristine, "uncontaminated" person vis-à-vis race in the first place: we are all hybrid. An impressive number of critical race theorists have argued cogently that there are no longer any originary identities or cultures, if in fact such things existed in the first place. As Stuart Hall puts it, "Fewer and fewer cultures are originary; fewer and fewer cultures can identify any lines of stable continuity between their origins and the present" ("Cultural" 176). That is, there is no such thing as a pure "race," a pure and distinct category of people unaffected by interaction on all kinds of levels with other peoples and other cultures, many with highly differentiated traditions, languages, values, and beliefs. This is not to suggest that there are no such things as national or cultural identities, only that because of the dizzying expansion of global institutions and technologies these identities and cultures are continually transculturally constituted and reconstituted in an unending, dynamic process. It would be more accurate to say that identities or cultures may be projected or imagined as unified, whole, and natural for strategic purposes of solidarity—although it may be a solidarity that nonetheless rallies around social markers such as language, skin color, or custom, for example. Edward Said says that because all populations, states, and groupings are *in fact* mixed,

> there cannot be any such thing as a pure race, a pure nation, or a pure collectivity, regardless of patriotic, ideological, or religious argument. A corollary to all this is that all efforts (particularly the efforts of governments or states) to purify one or several of these agglomerations are tantamount to organized discrimination or persecution: the examples of Nazi Germany and South Africa argue the force of such a judgement with considerable authority in today's world. (41)

Furthermore, race theorists such as Kwame Anthony Appiah, Jan Nederveen Pieterse, and Henry Louis Gates Jr. observe that biologists and other scientists have long known that the idea of a distinct race is indefensible on scientific grounds.

It is important, therefore, to understand the critical potential of hybridity for frustrating and thinking beyond old and static ideas of racial identities, for challenging the powerful fictions of race and older, restrictive forms of identity politics. As Robert Elliot Fox puts it, "'race'" thinking is a form of dementia, a dull desperate dreaming into sameness" (10). That is, while race represents a politics of difference, a kind of ideology of difference, it is nonetheless enacted in order to reproduce "the same," to keep "us" and "them" in ("our"/"their") place(s). Hybridity as a deliberate strategy that seeks to frustrate pristine racial categories represents a threat to that reproduction, to that sameness, to its formidable and fictional power. Hybridization involves more, however, than eating ethnic foods or sharing exotic stories and experiences; such a position, typical of much uncritical multiculturalism, still posits originary elements that are merely traded or shared, but not "translated," often within highly asymmetrical power relations. Theories of hybridity can help to nuance our analyses of how social identities are formed, reformed, and transformed and help us to better realize how culture and identity work not by perfectly reproducing themselves into infinity, but precisely by *translating between*" (Hall, "Cultural" 177).

Anzaldúa discusses a similar process of negotiation and hybridization that frustrates fictions of pristine social and cultural identities. She talks of what she calls a "*mestiza* consciousness," a borderland identity formed, in her case, at the juncture of various North American and Central American cultures. Drawing on the insights of Nancy Morejón, AnnLouise Keating calls this strategy of hybridization "*mestizaje* transculturation," a strategy intended to defy static notions of cultural purity by emphasizing the "mutually constituted and constantly changing nature of all racialized identities" (915–16). Such a consciousness is characterized by a tolerance for ambivalence and contradiction. In this view, ambivalence becomes a strategy to work against the settling effect of narrow and monologic notions of identity; it is a way to break down, as Anzaldúa says, the subject-object duality that keeps people prisoners of reductionist and dualistic definitions of themselves. Bhabha, too, thinks of ambivalence as an important tool of theoretical speculation because it implies an "agonistic, unresolved moment of transition" ("Staging" 12).

For Bhabha and Anzaldúa, hybridization—the deliberate emphasis on and strategic exploitation of the "in-between" moments of social and linguistic translation—becomes a way to think of resistance as an action, as an act of agency rather than as mere reaction. Anzaldúa perhaps says it most eloquently:

> It is not enough to stand on the opposite river bank, shouting questions, challenging patriarchal, white conventions. A

counterstance locks one into a duel of oppressor and oppressed; locked in mortal combat, like the cop and the criminal, both are reduced to a common denominator of violence. The counterstance refutes the dominant culture's views and beliefs, and, for this, it is proudly defiant. All reaction is limited by, and dependent on, what it is reacting against. Because the counterstance stems from a problem with authority—outer as well as inner—it's a step towards liberation from cultural domination. But it is not a way of life. . . . The possibilities are numerous once we decide to act and not react. (78–79)

Hybridity as a strategy for resisting thinking of identities as simple and restrictive represents the kind of resistance that Anzaldúa talks about: resistance as creative action and not mere reaction. For example, much "black" rhetoric of liberation was historically oppositional, formed in reaction to white domination. The nature of such domination made the development and expression of such oppositional discourse an imperative for survival. However, such discourse became something else, something new, something that exploited the transformed elements of cultural interaction. Otherwise, what happens to oppositional positions is that they become locked into patterns of reaction and are continually defined by what they are reacting against, by what they presumably are not. Resistance traditionally conceived as dualistic and oppositional does not allow for a departure from patterns and cycles of reaction that define identity and often involve violence. Thinking of resistance as more of a hybridization and as a translation, as a transformation of cultural codes and elements into something new and different, as a form of critical negotiation, allows us to think beyond the simple coming or putting together of two or more originary elements. Hybridity might be thought of more productively as an act of "translation" that occurs at the level of subject formation and as a strategy that exploits the doubleness of the inscriptive act. Such a strategy has the capability to disarticulate what we thought was originary, such as older forms of racial identity, and to rearticulate them along more positive and more complex lines. Like critical negotiation itself, hybridization is a strategy of border pedagogy, one that works to create complex and nuanced understandings of human subjectivities. Such a border pedagogy, as Henry Giroux puts it, works to "further create borderlands in which diverse cultural resources allow for the fashioning of new identities within existing configurations of power" (28).[1]

## A Critical Theory of Negotiation

The guiding problem of negotiation, then, is how to balance optimism with critique, how to remain hopeful about the possibility of doing more than simply expressing our differences while avoiding and resisting the colonizing strategies of negotiation that are disguised as civil discourse. Clearly, what is needed is to supplement these stances with a theory of "critical negotiation," an idea of negotiation that comes to resemble more a borderland dialogic process or an ethics of social and political engagement and less a mere "dealing." Such a theory of critical negotiation would do the following:

1) recognize the role and effect of emotion during negotiation and realize that, in fact, one of the intentions of traditional forms of negotiation is to dismiss emotion and discredit the role of the affective in rhetorical, political, and social exchange,

2) understand that negotiation is a co-constitutive process, that it is at the point of negotiation, of interaction, that meaning and identity are mutually constituted; and conceive of negotiation as a process of identity formation and as a strategy of hybridization that may be deployed in order to rearticulate meaning and identity, and that the rearticulation of identity and of meaning are connected to social change,

3) realize that how power relations are perceived before negotiation affects what happens during negotiation and influences whether and how critical transformative moments will be exploited, and

4) insist on situating negotiation within its larger social and historical contexts—being aware, for example, of the influence on negotiation of asymmetrical social and political relations stemming from sexual orientation, nationality, profession, ethnicity, gender, class, race, and age.

It might be useful at this point to look closely at these four characteristics of critical negotiation.

*The Role of the Affective in Critical Negotiation*
A theory of critical negotiation would recognize that emotion plays a vital role in the formation and transformation of social relations—as both an impetus for change and as a factor that influences political and rhetorical

interaction along and across lines of nationality, sexuality, ethnicity, gender, class, race, and age. It positions us to resist thinking of negotiation as a purely functional, rational, civil operation. This is not to say that negotiation and rhetorical exchange need necessarily regress to shouting matches where nothing is accomplished; rather, it is to say that we understand that negotiation defined simply along the lines of rationality, civility, and decorum is a specific and "interested" convention of interaction—largely institutional, parliamentary, and liberal—that deemphasizes the transformative potential of emotion. Bhabha says, "The discourse of political action and political choice has concentrated too much on questions of interest and too little on questions of political passion" ("Staging" 34). Because the *raison d'être* of negotiation has been the mediation of social, political, and market interests, it has allowed no rhetorical space for the expression of "political passion." We can certainly argue whether or not the expression of such passion is appropriate at specific kinds of negotiations. But a strictly functionalist and civil notion of social and political interaction does not allow for the study of the strong affective charge that lies at the heart of many of today's politics of difference and community. We need to recognize the influences of such affective charges if we are to begin to theorize the important role that emotion plays in dissensus politics and the construction of community. Bhabha says, a "history of affect as well as an affective history are very important tasks for the future" ("Staging" 35). In addition, it is important to see how the act of translation as the rearticulation of social and cultural codes works on a deep affective level. That is, translation in this sense is not simply an intellectual activity, a changing of minds, but one that involves modifying the ways we *feel* about one another, a move that requires intense reflection on the affective relations and politics of difference. All politics, according to Mouffe, operate to some degree on the affective level. In short, it would serve us well, especially in discussions about how to live with and respect our differences, to study and better understand the role and effect of what Peter Lyman refers to as the "paralanguages of emotion" in social, political, and rhetorical interaction.[2]

*Negotiation as Mutually Constitutive*
A theory of critical negotiation would make clear that the act of negotiation is mutually constitutive and not simply a trading of positions because such a realization allows for critical intervention. The "translation" involved in negotiation, like that involved in hybridity, posits that meaning is co-constituted or mutually inscribed at the moment of enun-

ciation or negotiation. Bhabha says that the most important thing about the process of enunciation as a kind of borderline concept is the awareness that it is through "the process of enunciation that the borders between objects or subjects or practices are being constituted" ("Staging" 19). Negotiation thought of as reconstitution and rearticulation disrupts thinking of negotiation strictly in the sense of parties' engaging in some kind of simple dealing with one another. For Bhabha, negotiation is always a "double-dealing"; that is, negotiation in a critical sense cuts both ways (25). There is, we might say, a doubleness to the inscriptive act, a process of mutual inscription. Also, Teresa Ebert talks of what she calls "rewriting," a critical act that seeks to change the meaning of words and social identities and, thus, social relations:

> "Rewriting" is a (post)modern strategy for what I call "activating" the "other" suppressed and concealed by dominant modes of knowing: it articulates the unsaid, the suppressed, not only of texts and signifying practices but also of the theories and frames of intelligibilities shaping them. Voicing this silenced "other" displaces the dominant logic—dislodging its hegemony and demystifying its "naturalness"—and unleashes alternative potential. (888)

Thought of as a kind of critical "double-dealing," negotiation need not follow the rules of simple civil trade or polite conversation. Further, thinking about negotiation as a critical, reflexive, (trans)formative process allows for dominant negotiating conventions themselves to be interrogated, critiqued, and, perhaps, changed.

### The Influence of Anteriority During Negotiation

A theory of critical negotiation stresses that, despite all appearances, subjects and their positions are not prefixed. The critical move here is to realize that the act of negotiation is a process of translation and rearticulation, a rewriting or reinscribing. To better realize the critical potential of translation or rearticulation, however, it is important to understand how what Bhabha refers to as "anteriority" works to create and sustain authority through negotiation:

> I think how you negotiate depends very much on how you read the weight and sedimentation of that prior fixing or prefixing of power or authority or domination. It's to try and rethink the context of that prefixing, to suggest that this prefixing may also be disarticulated

or unfixed, that I've always suggested lets us think about the moment of prefixing as a kind of anteriority that does itself in the present—in the moment when you're negotiating—produce its kind of anteriority. That's how I also want to try and rethink the *pre*; the *pre* is not a givenness, but an anteriority. ("Staging" 23–24)

Because subjects and meanings exist before negotiation, because they are anterior to it, does not mean that they are "pregiven." It is important to realize that pregivenness or prefixing is a kind of anteriority that does its work in the present; subjects and meanings in part emerge in enuciative, co-constitutive moments. That is, what we think of as pregiven is constituted as such in part in the present, during interaction and negotiation. For example, identities and institutions that present themselves as authoritatively prefixed solidify their very prefixedness by negotiating or struggling for, by "winning" that position to some extent *in the present*. Such prefixedness does not actually have the pregiven status that it seems; this is what Bhabha calls anteriority: a *sense* of pregivenness, the weight and authority of seeming to preexist, re-created continually in the present. Such a strategy is a mechanism of power, one that creates and sustains social and rhetorical authority. In this view, negotiation can become more than a mere process of dealing or compromise; it can become a struggle to expose the strategies of authorization of that which presents itself as (pre)given or natural. The objective of thinking of negotiation as "double-dealing" is to reveal and exploit the mutually constitutive dimensions of interaction that are concealed by functionalist notions of negotiation as the trading of pre-given meanings, objects, or identities. In terms of critical negotiation, hybridity, then, is not simply a condition of existence but a way of thinking about social identity and cultural meaning as not pregiven. This line of thinking needs to be exploited if we are to advance negotiation as something more than a willingness to compromise, as an art of the deal—as an attempt merely to make parties *feel* as if they got a "good deal." Clearly this is an unsatisfactory model for social and political interaction and the engagement of difference.

*The Histories and Contexts of Negotiation*
A theory of critical negotiation situates negotiation within its larger social and historical contexts—so that we can see, for example, how negotiation has been, and still is, used as a strategy of colonial and neocolonial domination that masks itself as functional and civil interaction. This is not to say that negotiation always operates this way, only that it is important to be on the alert for attempts to dehistoricize it. By bracketing the

histories and contexts of negotiation, we also do not attend to the motivations of those calling for it. Negotiation as a strategy to work things out is not inherently insidious, but it certainly may be used, and has been, to suppress action and deflect the trajectories of unsanctioned thinking. In this sense, negotiation is often a highly conservative and supremely stabilizing endeavor, a kind of civil dialogue that, as Mark Kingwell says, has no "critical bite" because it pretty much *"leaves everything as it is"*:

> Civil dialogue comes into play only when real power relations are no longer up for grabs—that is, when social roles are already highly defined and immune from routine questions about their legitimacy. It is also no coincidence that civil behavior has in the past been the preserve of the rich and powerful; they are the ones who can afford to indulge in good manners, who do not have to be rude to get what they want. Civility is, on this view, *both* evidence of deep-running colonizing strategies, by which persons (or groups) in a superior position maintain that position vis-à-vis some other persons (or groups), *and* the medium by which such hierarchies are maintained. Linguistic colonization is both a reflection and an instance of the more general social and political colonization effected between persons or groups. It is an unlikely place to look for the dialogue that may achieve justice. (236)

The histories and contexts of negotiation provide valuable lessons for using negotiation either in a pragmatic sense or as a guiding metaphor to work with and (re)write our differences.

In short, we must be cautious not to fetishize negotiation or treat it as a panacea, much as we have treated other liberal concepts such as tolerance and community. For example, Herbert Marcuse has argued that liberal definitions of tolerance are "repressive," that tolerance is always somebody's version of it, that it is not universal or "pure," and that it actually can hide inequitable power relations. Joseph Harris has shown how the notion of community has been similarly (mis)used. In much the same way, we might cultivate a healthy suspicion of negotiation to supplement the theories of negotiation in critical discourse.

### Negotiation as Transformative Action: Changing the Rules

As a kind of civil dialogue, negotiation is characterized by willingness to compromise; and because this willingness to compromise is based on moral acceptability and technical usefulness, it is presumed in much liberal thinking to be shared by all groups. Negotiation reconceived as critical negotiation—as what Iain Chambers calls "mutual interrogation," or what might also be called "mutual inscription"—attends to the politics of interaction and engagement that are necessary if we are to do more than merely express or negotiate our differences. Further, critical negotiation or mutual inscription allows for the realization that some parties may not be interested in compromise so as to maintain the status quo, and that others might be interested instead in disrupting and transforming the status quo. Chambers writes,

> To hold on to the uncertainties of mutual interrogation is impera-
> tive. Otherwise my desire continues to reproduce the cycles of
> hegemony that subject the other to *my* categories, to *my* need for
> alterity. Then my recognition of difference merely becomes the
> prison for the object of my desire. Requested to carry the burden
> of "authenticity," of "difference," of "post-coloniality," the other
> continues to be exploited, to be colonized, in another name. I am
> referring to what unfolds towards me and away from me, to what
> both envelops and exceeds me. (54)

What is productive about Chambers' stance is that it acknowledges the transformative potential of the otherness of the other, or what Teresa Ebert refers to as the alternative potential of the suppressed other (888). It also highlights the "double-dealing" aspect of negotiation that Bhabha talks about, the mutual constitution that occurs during social and cultural translation. Critical negotiation or mutual inscription helps us to recognize the need, if we are not merely to tolerate but to learn from and live with our differences, for dominant positions to be altered by the unknowable of other positions. Whereas traditional understandings of negotiation are characterized by a willingness to compromise, understandings of mutual critique are characterized by uncertainty and risk. Whereas traditional notions of negotiation are invested in maintaining the status quo, critical negotiation realizes that strong critique may serve as an impetus to upset the status quo. A theory of mutual inscription involves an understanding of social relations as dependent on the need to foster states of knowledge that are prepared to suffer modification and interrogation by what they neither possess nor can claim as their own (Chambers 50).

Calls for negotiation that do not critically examine the historical and political dimensions of negotiation leave open the possibility of reenacting those strategies of negotiation that have been used to colonize, displace, and dominate the disenfranchised. That is why a form of critical negotiation could be used productively in cultural studies and rhetorical theory as a way to create a sense of unease—not unease for its own sake but for the sake of not letting interpretations of social relations get too congealed into "the way things are." Such a way of thinking about negotiation is not simply a matter of identifying and communicating across borders, but rather a matter of realizing that borders and identities are co-constituted, and that there is a certain social authority that comes from the power to mask these very mutually constitutive dimensions of social relations. Negotiation as it is being talked about in discussions of cultural theory and difference needs to be critiqued, complexified, and used with some caution. The last thing we should want to do is to fetishize negotiation, to unproblematically respect the rhetorical politics and strategies of dominant groups, to call for and enact forms of "colonization" that seek to manage difference by insisting that people "show their cards" at the negotiating table.

# Chapter Two

## Rewriting the Difference of Race

> Race is an inevitable feature of the classroom; it is the
> ineluctable product of the racialization of American
> society. To expect that the classroom will somehow be
> exempt from the racialized meanings that are exploding
> in our culture is to have a sort of pedagogical naivete that
> is not only insular but is also destructive. Race belongs in
> the classroom where it belongs in society. . . . Race is part
> and parcel of the very fabric of the American intellectual
> project and also at the heart of the American project of
> democracy and self-discovery. We would be well-served
> to be more explicit about it and, therefore, to take it into
> account rather than allow it to inform our debates from a
> distance. By informing our debates from a distance, we
> do not get a chance to theorize race, we do not get a
> chance to explore race, we do not get a chance to demy-
> thologize racist power to hurt and harm us precisely
> because it is excluded from our explicit articulations.
>
> —Michael Eric Dyson

Some of the more urgent guiding problems for scholars of rhetoric and culture continue to concern how to teach, how to discuss, and how to represent cultural differences in ways that do not avoid issues of social, political, and material inequality. For about the last quarter of the twentieth century, questions of cultural difference have been posed largely through the institutional discourse of multiculturalism, a dis-

27

course that typically posits a "multicultural society" in terms of diversity and pluralism, a society of diverse yet distinct groups or cultures interacting and living among one another. At its best, multiculturalism is an extension of the civil rights political movement and, as such, has proven valuable in increasing awareness of and respect for the needs and interests of historically disenfranchised groups. However, because much multicultural discourse continues to represent difference *as diversity*, it often advances pedagogies and curricular reform that elide histories of difference *as alterity*, as the politics of "othering" people for particular reasons. That is, one of the more crucial shortcomings of uncritical multiculturalism is that in its celebration and respect for cultural differences it typically does not inquire into genealogies of difference, or the historical production of cultural differences. Multiculturalism often works from a kind of historical amnesia, a way of thinking about cultures as discrete and pristine social items that live "unsullied by the intertextuality of their historical locations" (Bhabha, *Location* 34).

Because multiculturalism emphasizes "accommodating diversity rather than examining how differences have been historically constructed," it often is complicit in "preserving ingrained beliefs and practices" concerning cultural difference (Mahala and Swilky 185–86). The most troublesome of these beliefs, as Dyson observes, is that all groups "have a relative equality of articulation within the space of American intellectual culture" (153). Much of this is the result of multiculturalism's tendency to shy way from the concept of race as an "ideology of difference" (Said), as a genealogy of difference, as one of the most historically fundamental politics of "othering." Indeed, a more explicit articulation of race as an ideology of difference can help to interrogate received notions of cultural difference, as well as act as a corrective to the easy-going versions of multicultural difference so prevalent today. Working toward more nuanced and historically informed understandings of race is to relearn *the difference of the difference* of race, we might say, to critically (re)negotiate its significance in contemporary culture. It is to better understand the historical constitution of cultural difference in order to rearticulate and redefine—or "rewrite," as Teresa Ebert would say—social identities in more complex and equitable terms than race has traditionally allowed.

To be sure, multiculturalism concerns itself with diversity and culture, and so it appears to deal with race. But race theory and multiculturalism are not interchangeable. If multiculturalism doesn't always posit race outright as a passive descriptor of natural categories of people, it certainly doesn't encourage a hermeneutics of race, as race theory does. According to many race theorists, race is not a passive descriptor of natural categories of people. It is a concept deeply enmeshed in New World histories of colonialism and slavery, in ways of "othering" people, of inscribing differences in cultural imaginaries and social institutions for the purpose of defining people for inclusion and exclusion, for defining who is eligible to receive rights and who isn't. In this view, race, like the interlocking concept of gender, is a supremely political and contested concept and is not a mere reflection of pregiven social relations. For this reason, there is a need to use historical analysis and critical theory to initiate "a better understanding of the ways in which *race* is used in particular social and historical contexts, what it signifies and its impact on social, political, economic and cultural processes in contemporary societies" (Solomos and Back xiv).

Viewing cultural and social difference as the result of social dynamics rather than simply as states of being has important implications for scholarship and for resisting understanding social identities in restrictive and reductive terms. Our differences cannot be accommodated merely by the curricular reforms of additive models of multiculturalism, by simply adding "others'" voices and texts into existing canonical and discriminatory structures. What is crucial is the encouragement of our differences—a critical negotiation—to change things, to influence imagination, and to redefine social institutions, in an ongoing hegemonic struggle over representations and terms of difference. Linda Brodkey argues that *curricular* reform (changing what we study) must be flanked by *pedagogical* reform (changing how and why we study), which includes "learning and teaching a theoretically recognizable and responsible version of difference" (195). Learning and teaching theoretically recognizable and responsible versions of difference must include theoretical and historical inquiries into past and emerging formations of race, what Michael Omi and Howard Winant call "racial projects," and their interconnections with other signs of difference such as nationality, sexuality, ethnicity, and gender. What is clearly needed then is a shift from naturalistic and scientific understandings of race to a hermeneutics of race wherein the significance of race to cultural difference is underscored rather than ignored.

## Misconceptions about Race

One of the best ways to initiate a hermeneutics of race is first to question the misconceptions about race that circulate in popular culture and elsewhere. In his introduction to *"Race," Writing, and Difference,* Henry Louis Gates, Jr. observes that although race has long been recognized as a fiction—albeit a powerful socio-political one with formidable effects— still "our conversations are replete with usages of race which have their sources in the dubious pseudoscience of the eighteenth and nineteenth centuries" (4). Gates elaborates:

> The sense of difference defined in popular usages of the term "race" has both described and *inscribed* differences of language, belief system, artistic tradition, and gene pool, as well as all sorts of supposedly natural attributes such as rhythm, athletic ability, cerebration, usury, fidelity, and so forth. The relation between "racial character" and these sorts of characteristics has been inscribed through tropes of race, lending the sanction of God, biology, or the natural order to even presumably unbiased descriptions of cultural tendencies and differences. (5)

Jan Nederveen Pieterse claims, however, that race thinking is now so outdated that "the very term 'race' is no longer tenable," that the "science of race" is routinely referred to as a pseudoscience. He continues, "still it may be easily overlooked that until fairly recently throughout the western world 'race thinking' was widespread, carried great authority and was widely regarded as scientific" (50).

Both scholars are accurate when they say that race refers to a way of thinking about social difference that rests on the "dubious pseudoscience" (at least by today's standards) of the eighteenth and nineteenth centuries. But, like Gates, I do not share Pieterse's optimism that thinking about cultural difference in outmoded racial terms is a thing of the past. Such ways of thinking about race that Gates describes pervade academic discussions as well as popular usage. AnnLouise Keating observes that theorists who attempt to "deconstruct 'race' often inadvertently reconstruct it by reinforcing the belief in permanent, separate racial categories," undercutting in the process their belief that race is a constantly changing sociohistorical concept and not a biological fact (902).[1]

We might say that a certain way of thinking about race has "set in" to American culture, making the hermeneutics of race all the more important. Thinking of groups of people as permanent, natural, and separate categories, as "races," also surfaces in the classroom. Often the problem is that racial thinking is a way of viewing cultural identity that interferes with productive dialogue on social and political issues. Students often make assumptions about other writers and other students—about their morals, their intelligence, their ability, their rhetorical ethos, and so on—based on their "race." In my experience, however, most students have superficial or hazy understandings of race, of what it signifies and represents. It is helpful, I have found, to discuss race as an ideological and structural social formation that has resulted from, and that continues to be shaped by, the contestation of historically situated "racial politics" precisely because many students continue to think of race as describing unchanging and unchangeable social identities. Interrogating race in this way encourages students to talk and write about social identity and cultural difference, as well as social and political issues, in historically and theoretically informed ways. My hope is for students to be able to engage and write about social tensions, ideological conflicts, and cultural differences at the same time minimizing their making hasty conclusions and broad generalizations about people's belief, attitudes, and social positionings.

But relearning the difference of race is not an easy task precisely because thinking about racial identities as identities that are discrete, static, and congealed continues to dominate academic and popular conceptions of cultural difference and is not a thing of the past as Pieterse asserts. (Relearning the difference of race is difficult, too, because of the affective relations of difference and affective investments, something I will talk about in Chapters 4 and 5.) Confusion over the meaning of race abounds in both popular and academic forums. Race is often used to mean anything from blood stock to culture to nationality to ethnicity—the meanings of which are themselves often highly contested and ill-defined. There is a real need to be critical of the terms and concepts that have come to define and constitute cultural difference, to see these terms and concepts as *signs of struggle* that influence how differences are conceived and deployed. Issues of representation must be understood in the context of specific historical moments characterized by particular *crises of meaning*, crises that have at their center how differences are used in order to define people for purposes of inclusion and exclusion and to identify those who are eligible to receive rights and privileges and those who are not. Struggles for definition are particularly evident over the meanings of concepts enmeshed in the constitution of cultural differences, such as, in this case, race.

By focusing on race as a politics of difference and by confronting misconceptions about race in the classroom, it is my hope that students come to understand that cultural differences and social relations are not merely a reflection of "the way things are" but are born out of interpretive and representational struggles. I have found it productive in the classroom to thematize race as what Said calls "an ideology of difference," an ideology that both informs and is enacted through particular social policies as a way of negatively valuing and stigmatizing people on the basis of their differences. Thinking about race in this way helps students to write and talk about cultural differences in historically and critically minded ways, and it encourages them to see that social and cultural differences are not a result of "the way things are" but instead are complex historically and politically constituted relationships.

## Why Focus on Difference when Studying Race?

To develop a hermeneutics of race, it is important also to view race as an ideology of difference enmeshed with other ideologies of difference, such as nationality, sexuality, and gender. The concept of difference, of course, has been discussed in critical and literary theory for some time. But it is crucial that those in rhetorical and cultural studies who are concerned with interrogating the construction of social identity and the formation of structures of social inequality continue to focus on difference precisely because humans have defined and continue to define one another by their differences. More than this, it is through "ideologies of difference" that people come to be marked negatively—not white, not European, not male, for example—in order to relegate their rights to an inferior or lesser status (Said 41). And while some differences in skin color or physical features, for example, may occur naturally, the characteristics and quali- ties ascribed to people on the basis of these differences do not; such ascription, that is, is not natural but political.

Also, our differences are not superficial; they have weight and depth. The idea that differences are superficial holds that although we have differences, they are surface and do not really matter: they do not matter because, as the argument goes, we are all really the same on the inside. Believing that we can end social strife and racial tension by focusing on our similarities, by merely accommodating and celebrating our differ- ences, not only discourages analysis of how people have been and continue to be defined negatively on the basis of their differences, but it also militates against our understanding the weight and depth of differ- ences, how differences are socially instituted and affectively inscribed into people's emotions, bodies, and minds beyond superficial levels of appearance. The so called "nervous liberal," for example, is more concerned with calming strife and tension by appeals to questionable similarities than in combating discrimination by engaging how difference has been used to define others reductively and negatively. In short, our differences *matter*; how they are conceived, defined, and discussed matters in how they affect social and political policy, in how they affect decisions about inclusion and exclusion, and in how they influence how people think and feel about one another. To counter racial discrimination, the moral politics of liberal pluralism would have us focus on our similarities (that we are all human, that we are all the same on the inside, that we should somehow see past our differences). This is not to dismiss real human similarities that encourage understanding, compassion, and empathy. Instead, it is to argue that appeals to human similarities are often spurious. Certainly, we can speak of having a common humanity—that we all experience things like suffering, loss, and joy, for example—but we do so differently, in ways that are inflected by both personal and cultural factors; in short, we can say without being contradictory that although there are common experiences, we experience them *differently*. Differences are inscribed in our hearts and minds; they do not stop at our skin. They influence the ways in which we think and feel about others and ourselves, and we avoid and ignore them at our peril.

Attempting to look beyond our differences to our (imagined) similarities as the only basis for understanding, compassion, and empathy discourages learning how to forge such human connections across the messy and gritty realities of difference. Focusing on difference also allows for the realization that the social and political dimensions of these differences are not natural or given but socially constructed and thus able to be rearticulated along more positive lines. As Said puts it, "One can declare oneself *for* difference (as opposed to sameness or homogenization) without at the same time being for the rigidly enforced and policed separation of populations into different groups" (40). In other words, one can declare oneself for the "right" to be different, and argue for a conception of the *civitas* based on difference and dissensus, not necessarily on conformity and uniformity.

Ebert contends that in order to continue to develop critical social theories based on concepts of difference, it is crucial to think of difference in terms other than the Derridean notion of a "free play of signifiers." Ebert argues that "differences are produced by social conflicts which usually privilege one set of differences in order to serve the interests of dominant social relations" (889). It is the project of critical theory, she continues, to rearticulate "the social struggles in which difference is inscribed in order to activate old and new sites of resistance, opposition, and change" (889). Such a way of thinking about and deploying difference is part of what Ebert refers to as "resistance postmodernism":

> I would like to articulate a resistance postmodernism that views the relation between word and world, language and social reality or, in short, "difference," not as the result of textuality but as the effect of social struggles. Language acquires its meaning not from its formal system, as Saussure proposes, but from its place in the social struggle over meanings. Names of racial groups, for instance, are not a consequence of the textual play of difference but the outcome of the struggles over the signifiers (names) and meanings used to make sense of these groups—as in the conflicts over the terms, "Negro," "Black," "African-American"—and their effects on the social situation of the racial other. Resistance postmodernism, thus, draws its linguistic theory not from Saussure but from Bakhtin and Voloshinov, who argued that the sign becomes an arena of social struggle. Out of this politicized difference, resistance postmodernists can build a new socially transformative politics of emancipation and freedom from gender, race, and class exploitation. (887)

In this view, "race" itself—as well as associated terms such as "white," "black," "African-American," and so on—can be seen as ideological signs, as "arenas of social struggle" that have material consequences. For example, the term "black" has been used historically as a discriminatory term to signify and identify something that is not "white," something that is not good, pure, right, normal. However, "black" has been reappropriated and redeployed in such a way as to contest those earlier definitions, to rearticulate positive self-definitions as well as coherent political agendas.

Omi and Winant argue for thinking of race in much the same way that Bhabha and Ebert argue for thinking of cultural difference. They suggest that because "there is a continuous temptation to think of race as an *essence*, as something fixed, concrete, and objective," and because there is also an opposite temptation to imagine race as "a mere *illusion*, a purely ideological construct which some ideal non-racist social order would eliminate," the effort must be made to understand race as "an unstable and 'decentered' complex of social meanings constantly being transformed by political struggle" (54–55). Taking such an approach to the study of difference and the meaning of race helps me, as Brodkey puts it, to instruct and support students in a "critique of received wisdom, which in their case, as in mine, means a sustained interrogation of the doxa out of which claims about reality arise and to which their claims and mine contribute" (161). That is, in order to counter thinking that suggests that cultural differences are simply a result of "the way things are" (the doxa out of which claims about reality arise), in the classroom I approach race and cultural difference as struggle concepts located in specific socio-historical moments. In this way, I want students to "test" their opinions—to which they never tire of telling me they have the "right"—against history and against theory in order to see that "their" opinions have roots in other discourses, that the way they "feel" about an issue at hand is an interested, biased, and partial account of things. My hope is that students begin to argue for their opinions and their differences in ways that are informed by histories or genealogies of difference. This, I have found, helps to discourage students from retreating to a "well-that's-just-my-opinion" position, a position undergirded by the politics of uncritical pluralism, and one that often ends argument and discourages analysis of the very kinds of politics of difference that must be taken into account.

## Racial Formation Theory and Racial Thinking

I have found Omi and Winant's "racial formation theory" helpful when thinking about and discussing race in the classroom, and I am using their ideas to help define a critical study of race, one that varies from a more formally defined "critical race theory" as the integration of race theory and critical legal studies. A critical theory of race based on racial formation theory is a field of critical inquiry (which may and often does include critical legal studies) that raises the issue of race as a crucial basis for the organization of society for at least the last three hundred or so years—from the production and distribution of wealth and the division of power to the construction of identities and ways of making sense of realities. Of course, other divisions of culture, especially class and gender, are deeply imbricated with racial divisions. Race theory, in this sense, starts by recognizing that "despite its uncertainties and contradictions, the concept of race continues to play a fundamental role in structuring and shaping the social world" and that it is part of the task of critical theory to trace and explain this (Omi and Winant 55). Omi and Winant's "racial formation theory" can be helpful to projects in cultural and rhetorical studies seeking to put critical pressure on those positions that argue that cultural differences are the result of natural or divine, and thus unchangeable, forces. Omi and Winant define *racial formation* as the "sociohistorical process by which racial categories are created, inhabited, transformed, and destroyed" (55). Racial formation, they argue, is a process of historically situated *racial projects* in which "human bodies and social structures are represented and organized" (56).

The cornerstone of racial thinking is a conception of difference as negative and binary. For example, being considered not-European has connoted historically a binary difference (us/them) wherein "others" (them) are negatively valued. Racial thinking is a way of thinking about cultural difference that is based on quasiscientific arguments of the eighteenth and nineteenth centuries, and increasingly on sociological and political arguments that continue to disguise their nature as such. Racial thinking classifies people as groups according to chromatic and morphological differences that come to represent cultural differences in tradition, belief, language, and custom as natural. That is, physical differences come to be seen as markers or signs of "natural" or "given" differences in ability, intelligence, inclination, aptitude, and so on. Furthermore, as Bhabha says, in the (re)production of these character-istics as markers of difference, the characteristics come to bear a whole set of significations, tensions, and anxieties; these characteristics then become the signs of those tensions and anxieties about cultural difference ("Staging" 16).

The problem with thinking about social identity in racial terms is that it gives way to uncomplicated and reductive explanations of people's identities, experiences, and realities. Thinking of social identities in racial terms and accepting the moral presuppositions that ground that kind of thinking must be resisted if arguments that discourage the right to be *variously* different are to be countered. Uncritical racial thinking is a way of thinking about cultural difference that does not question the ideological formation of race, that encourages people to believe in the fictions of pristine social identities, and that does not see race as a historical mechanism of negative differentiation.

The color-blindness promoted both by liberals, who want to see beyond difference, and by those of the political right, who declare that we have moved beyond exploiting people on the basis of racial difference, represents a blindness to the historical, social, and political formations of the differencing effects of race, as well as to those differences that matter: those of social, political, and economic inequity. Sociologist Ruth Frankenberg calls this color-blindness "power-evasiveness," highlight-ing that what is evaded or ignored is not simply difference based on skin color but the actual power dynamics and asymmetrical political relations that come to be "papered over" and represented by skin color (*White* 14). The different forms of color-blindness advocated by liberals and neoconservatives discourage seeing race as a powerful form of devaluing differences, a form not only with distinct historical trajectories but one that is so indistinct at the same time that its very slipperiness allows it to be used for all sorts of discrimination, including those forms appealing to civilization, nationality, morality, biology, culture, and blood. Because of this slipperiness, we would be well-served, as Dyson says, to theorize and explore race rather than rely on multicultural platitudes that reassure us that everything will be okay if we just realize that we are all the same on the inside. Not only is it crucial to be aware of the historical trajectories of race, it would also serve us and our students well to be able to map the contemporary manifestations of racism in order to resist its negative and discriminatory effects and to work to create social identities that are more complexly, creatively, and trans-culturally defined. In this way, we resist thinking of people in negative terms (by what they are not or by what they lack), and consequently we clear rhetorical and political space for effective rearticulations of individual and group identities.

Scholars of race such as Omi and Winant, Anthony Appiah, Henry Louis Gates, Ellis Cose, Michael Dyson, Benjamin DeMott, and bell hooks—to name only a few—believe that at a time when thinking about race and racial issues needs to be at its keenest and most nuanced, it is characterized by benign tolerance, avoidance, silence, and apathy. These scholars also observe that discussions about race are often paralyzed by denial and derailed by invective. More than this, there is a pressing need to continually define racism in explicitly social and political terms in order to counter organic and individualistic interpretations of racism that help to deemphasize the extent of its systematic institution. That is, racism is often defined in organic terms: as a sickness curable either by prescriptive measures or by letting it run its course. It is also often defined in strictly individual terms: as a supremely individual condition, as being perpetuated by a few reprehensible sociopaths. In such cases, whites are often all too eager to denounce other whites as racist, thereby denying any possible complicity in racist social structures (they believe) and freeing them of the unpleasant rigors of self-analysis. Both individualizing racism and seeing it as an organic phenomenon reinforce patterns of thinking that posit that race no longer plays a fundamental role in structuring and representing the social world, that race is a "misconception left over from the past, and suitable now only for the dustbin of history" (Omi and Winant 55). What is needed, then, is a model of historical inquiry and critical analysis that can inform classroom discussions of and writing on race and cultural difference. That is, writing instructors and students need not talk and write about race as if differences do not exist, nor do discussions need to escalate to name-calling and finger-pointing. Part of my objective is to help students come to see themselves as writers who, as Brodky puts it, have a "vested interest in particular discursive representations and who recognize that in the context of the course, at least, the highest value is placed on complicated rather than simplified representations of human subjectivity" (203). Focusing on race as a social and political concept that greatly influences subjectivity and consciousness in conjunction with other social categories such as gender is a way to counter racial thinking and begin to complexify understandings of cultural identities and experience.[2]

## The Study of Whiteness and Race Traitoring

So how we do escape the "bounds of race," as Dominick LaCapra calls them, the accreted histories of racial thinking and the only half-dead remains of colonial ideology that continue to inform our understandings of cultural difference? It has been my argument that we can never really think outside of race but that we can make ourselves and our students aware of some of the ways that race operates differently in different contexts and that we can work toward more complex and positive understandings of cultural differences. There is, of course, a rich critical and literary history of African-American resistance to the traditional restrictive definitions of race. But what I want to do here is to trace some emerging studies of the cultural signification of whiteness and explore how such studies can help to counter traditional racial thinking. Critical studies of whiteness (studies of what it means to be considered "white," studies of the construction of whiteness as a social category) and race traitoring represent emergent ways that whites in particular can begin to counter racist thinking and racist discourse. Studies of whiteness and race traitoring both use critical theory and historical analysis and do not seek to deny or ignore economic and political differences between groups but seek to place these differences at the center of analysis. For this reason, these projects offer productive directions for writing about and studying race and cultural difference in rhetorical and cultural studies. Studies of whiteness might act as a supplement to recent scholarship concerned with those issues stemming from discussions of cultural difference and contact, ideological conflict, and dissensus pedagogy.

For the past several years, theorists in cultural and literary studies have been examining how what we call "white" subjectivities are generally built around silences about the cultural signification of whiteness itself. Keating argues that whiteness is a "constantly changing sociohistorical concept" that maintains cultural legitimacy by "dominant culture's inability or reluctance to see it as such" (902, 905). Whiteness often is not regarded as a sociohistorical or political concept but rather as describing a natural, singular racial identity. Because whiteness is unmarked it becomes the unrecognized and unacknowledged norm by which the cultural validity of "others" is measured. That is, how whiteness is culturally and ideologically constructed and maintained and how it in turn affects the production of categories such as "other" or "black," for example, are rarely interrogated. As Kobena Mercer has argued, whiteness and its "violent denial of difference" serve a vital function in masking social and economic inequalities in contemporary Western cultures (206). Keating puts it this way: "By negating those people—whatever the color of their skin—who do not measure up to 'white' standards, 'whiteness' has played a central role in maintaining and naturalizing a hierarchical social system and a dominant/subordinate worldview" (902).

Studies of the cultural signification of whiteness represent recent and effective ways for whites in particular to counter racism, and some of the more productive ways to extend critical race theory in general. Although Keating thinks that these studies cannot be dismissed as the latest scholarly fad in academia's publish or perish game, still, as Frankenberg writes in the introduction to *Displacing Whiteness*, there is a "risk that in undertaking intellectual work on whiteness one might contribute to processes of recentering it, as well as reifying the term and its 'inhabitants'" (1). Such studies, then, must be undertaken self-reflexively, for there are tremendous risks, writes Frankenberg, *in not* critically engaging whiteness:

> Among these are, first, a continual failure to displace the "unmarked marker" status of whiteness, a continued inability to "color" the seemingly transparency of white positionings. Second, to leave whiteness unexamined is to perpetuate a kind of asymmetry that has marred even many critical analyses of racial formation and cultural practice. Here the modes of alterity of everyone-but-white-people are subjected to ever more meticulous scrutiny, celebratory or not, while whiteness remains unexamined—un-

qualified, essential, homogenous, seemingly self-fashioned, and apparently unmarked by history or practice. Third, critical attention to whiteness offers a ground not only for an examination of white selves (who may indeed be white *others*, depending on the position of the speaker) but also for the excavation of the foundations of *all* racial and cultural positionings. (*Displacing* 1–2)

The crucial move of whiteness studies is the placement of the social construction of whiteness and white subjectivities squarely in the realm of race theory and critical study in order to better analyze how whiteness operates in the structuring of racial alterity and cultural consciousness.

The study of whiteness clearly has implications for critical race theory and for cultural and rhetorical studies concerned with politics of difference. As Henry Giroux writes in "Racial Politics and the Pedagogy of Whiteness,"

Analyzing "whiteness" as a central element of racial politics becomes useful in exploring how "whiteness" as a cultural practice promotes race-based hierarchies, how white racial identity structures the struggle over cultural and political resources, and how rights and responsibilities are defined, confirmed, or contested across diverse racial claims. "Whiteness" in this context becomes less a matter of creating a new form of identity politics than an attempt to rearticulate "whiteness" as part of a broader project of cultural, social, and political citizenship. (295)

As Giroux notes, the critical study of whiteness should not be about creating a new form of "white" identity politics, something that would be anathema to the critical study of race in postmodern times because it has the potential to slip toward white supremacy. Rather, the critical study of whiteness should be about providing

some insights into how "whiteness" as a cultural practice is learned through the representation of racialized identities and into how students might critically mediate the complex relations between "whiteness" and racism, not by having them repudiate their "whiteness," but by grappling with its racist legacy and its potential to be rearticulated in oppositional and transformative terms, to move beyond a view of "whiteness" as simply a trope of domination. (296)

Giroux goes on to discuss a pedagogy of whiteness that does not privilege, reify, or recenter but rather analyzes and decenters white subjectivities.

The point is not to repudiate whiteness but, as Giroux says, to grapple with its racist legacy, to rearticulate it in transformative terms, and to move beyond a view of whiteness as simply a trope of domination. He offers helpful directions toward a pedagogy of whiteness, and he discusses how he uses the films *Dangerous Minds* and *Suture* in his classroom interrogations of whiteness.

The popular and widely appealing *Dangerous Minds*, he argues, presents a version of whiteness that is unreflexive and reinforces the "highly racialized, though reassuring, mainstream assumption that chaos reigns in inner-city public schools and that white teachers alone are capable of bringing order, decency, and hope to those on the margins of society" (304). The popularity of this kind of liberal white paternalism as an answer to racial problems clearly should be thematized, critiqued, and avoided. While *Suture* breaks with "the Hollywood cinematic tradition of presenting 'whiteness' as an 'invisible' though determining discourse," it does not offer a model of reconstruction, a way to think of whiteness as something other than merely a "trope of domination" (306). Still, because *Suture* highlights racial politics in general and whiteness particularly as a socially constructed category of identification, it has potential to initiate discussion about how whiteness acts as an invisible cultural yardstick by which "others" are measured and judged in American society.

Critically studying whiteness has led me to reconceive one of my assignments using Sharon Olds' poem "On the Subway" to discuss and write about racial issues. In "Beyond Dissensus: Exploring the Heuristic Value of Conflict," I discuss how I used the poem in conjunction with other texts, such as Carole J. Sheffield's "Sexual Terrorism" and Brent Staples' "Black Men in Public Space." My hope was for students to think and write honestly about race and to see the intricate connections between gender and race. In the article, I describe the poem as an example of the kind of "honest confrontation" that bell hooks thinks is necessary for us to begin to take responsibility for examining our own responses to and involvement in race and gender relations that must accompany any critical social dialogue (*Teaching* 106). I have had some success in discussing with students the complex intersections of race and gender. But thinking about the poem from a stance of critical whiteness studies, I have come to realize that the poem is less an "honest confrontation" and more a meditation on "liberal guilt." At the crucial ethical moment, the "white" narrator realizes that she has been making stereotypical assumptions about the "black" "boy" sitting across from her in the subway car: that he is a mugger, that he is poor. At this crucial moment, the narrator muses,

"And he is black/and I am white, and without meaning or/trying to I must profit from his darkness." And later, she feels, "There is/no way to know how easy this/white skin makes my life" (5).

True: it is difficult to measure the affective dimensions of racism, and complete empathy is unachievable. But what "whites" can do to counter racism is to examine and counter the ways that, "without meaning to," they profit from associating people with negative representations of "darkness" and "blackness," how "whiteness" profits from its positive differentiation from "blackness." In Olds' poem, the transformative potential of the ethical moment is lost in a defeated sense of liberal guilt: racism is everywhere, it must be terrible for those who endure it, and I'm part of it. While this is where the poem ends, it is, of course, where critical interrogations of race and whiteness should begin: with examining and rhetoricizing the often invisible politics of alterity. Otherwise, the real work of interrogating social, political, and economic differences is never engaged, much like when students end dialogue and critique when they claim, "Well, that's just my opinion." In other words, identifying racism and recognizing some amorphous, unconscious complicity is not the same thing as critical, active projects of antiracism, of creative and reflexive ways of interrogating and countering racism.

In our emerging interrogations of whiteness, we must continue to ask, as Mike Hill suggests in the introduction to his collection, *Whiteness: A Critical Reader*, "What does whiteness want?" In other words, we cannot let what he calls "white writing" act like another form of "white noise," as a way of excluding the writing of others and establishing yet another privileged discourse in the white spaces of institutional and academic forums. White studies must remain self-critical and self-reflexive if they are not to become a last ditch effort on the part of white academic culture to square off an area of discourse to again exclude "others" from knowledge production and from defining the terms of debates over social difference. That is, critical studies of whiteness should be about "critical negotiation," about rearticulating whiteness as part of a broader project of cultural, social, and political citizenship by examining its racist legacy and by positing self-critical and positive white identities that are not paralyzed by guilt or denial.

Race traitoring, a theoretical/activist movement, is another emerging way that whites can, in this case, "abolish" racism. Through their journal *Race Traitor* (the first five issues of which have now been collected as a book) and their editorials and manifestos, John Garvey and Noel Ignatiev call for nothing less than "the abolition of the white race," what they call "the new abolitionism." Their motto: "Treason to whiteness is loyalty to humanity" ("Toward" 346). Their general theoretical stance works from ideas we have already seen: that race, and in this case the "white" race, is socially constructed and thus can be, in their words, "undone." However, Garvey and Ignatiev differ radically from Giroux and others who think that "whiteness" can be rearticulated and transformed from a trope of domination by resisting its historical and contemporary connections to white colonialism and white supremacy. They write, "advocating the abolition of the white race is distinct from what is called 'antiracism'" ("Abolish" 10). This distinction is based on radical identification with those who experience racism and on the utopian belief that racism can be abolished rather than merely hegemonically struggled against. They see the white race as a "club that enrolls certain people at birth, without their consent, and brings them up according to its rules. For the most part the members go through life accepting the benefits of membership, without thinking about the costs": the misery and poverty of others ("Abolish" 10). To dissolve the club would mean "white people's responding to every manifestation of white supremacy as if it were directed against them" ("Toward" 349). The idea of race traitoring, of course, echoes Marx's idea of class traitors, those intellectuals who would commit class suicide and "defect" to the working class to help with its liberation.

What I like about this stance is that it thematizes race as a continuing form of economic and political exploitation, that there is a price for "club" membership that the members themselves do not pay. Although I am drawn to the idealistic enthusiasm of this position (that white racism can be overcome by an ongoing campaign of individual and collective breaks with white solidarity traditionally conceived), still I agree with Omi and Winant that race—and, thus, whiteness—is a concept that cannot be dissolved completely but that must be rearticulated or critically negotiated hegemonically within cultural and political fields. And I agree with Giroux that whiteness is not inherently a bad thing to be completely done away with, nor can the negative legacies of whiteness genuinely be disinherited and disowned.

Robert Elliot Fox talks about the possibility of a shift in consciousness, of becoming what he calls "post-white": "Since whiteness is not an 'essence' but a construct, it isn't given but has to be acquired. Therefore, one can refuse to (seek to) acquire it. If whiteness must reproduce itself each generation, then one can refuse to reproduce it" (12). Generally, he agrees with Keating that what is needed is an assault on "white" ideology. I think post-whiteness (a critical process of identity formation that critiques and affirms at the same time) is a helpful direction to aim for but one surely that is not easy to achieve because it takes, at the very least, intense attention to transforming white identities. But the major problem with *Race Traitor's* and Fox's proposal to refuse simply to acquire whiteness is that, as Linda Alcoff says,

> In one important sense, whites cannot disavow whiteness [or, similarly, simply refuse it]. One's appearance of being white will still operate to confer privilege in numerous and significant ways, to avow treason does not render whites ineligible for these privileges, even if they work hard to avoid them. ("What" 17)

Perhaps a better way for whites to work to achieve what we might call "post-white" identities, white identities that are critical of but that do not ignore connections to the positive and negative aspects of past white identities, is for whites to develop their own form of double consciousness. Working from ideas of W.E.B. Du Bois, Alcoff suggests that perhaps white identity needs to develop its own sense of double consciousness:

> For whites, double consciousness requires an ever present acknowledgment of the historical legacy of white identity constructions in the persistent structures of inequality and exploitation, as well as a newly awakened memory of the many white traitors to white privilege who have struggled to contribute to the building of an inclusive human community.... The legacy of European-based cultures is a complicated one. It is better approached through a two-sided analysis than an argument that obscures either its positive or negative aspects. White representations of multiculturalism must then be similarly dialectical, retrieving from obscurity the history of white antiracism even while providing a detailed account of colonialism and its many cultural effects. ("What" 25)

Du Bois spoke of the divided consciousness or "two-ness" of African-American identity, of the difficult disjunctures created by democratic ideals of being American and the realities of being "Negro." The two-ness of white identity must account for the operation of whiteness in the history of which Du Bois speaks while it must attempt to achieve post-whiteness, a critique of the negative aspects of whiteness and a (re)affirmation of its positive ones. Generally, I think that these kinds of "inside jobs"—"race suicide" and interrogation of white identity formation—combined with intense attention to white identity transformation can help to forge social identities that aid in the erosion of fixed categories of color, ones that are not predicated on negative, binary thinking.

## Trading in Old Ideas

Because race is a flexible concept, it has been used throughout history as the basis of discrimination, displacement, dislocation, and slavery—often buttressed by the religious, scientific, and/or social theories of the time. And although the concept of race is connected to specific historical and social contexts, it is nonetheless often thought of as describing social identities in essential, biological, or God-given terms. For this reason, it is necessary for scholars of rhetoric and culture to pay close attention to critical race theory and the changing dimensions of ideologies of difference. We cannot be satisfied with merely deconstructing race, as some argue. Howard Winant writes,

> Race is a condition of individual and collective identity, a permanent, though tremendously flexible, element of social structure. Race is a means of knowing and organizing the social world; it is subject to continual contestation and reinterpretation, but it is no more likely to disappear than any other form of human inequality and difference. . . . To rethink race is not only to recognize its permanence, but also to understand the essential test that it poses for any diverse society seeking to achieve a modicum of freedom. (xiii)

That is, as a process of cultural differentiation, race, like gender, will not simply go away, cannot be wished away, nor will it somehow become irrelevant in the United States and the larger global context.

The point is that we cannot think outside terms such as race; it simply has too much historical and institutional drag. However, we can struggle to rearticulate and to redefine social identities in more complex and equitable terms than race has traditionally allowed. And because race continues to "color" perceptions of people negatively, it is important for cultural and rhetorical theory to be critical of racial thinking in any form that it may take, for there is still much of it going on all over the world today—not only in the United States but in Eastern Europe, the Middle East, Africa, Ireland, and Southeast Asia. And because these "ideologies of difference" have important implications for how we and students argue and write about cultural difference—for questioning the *doxa* out of which claims to truth arise, for educational policy, for pedagogy—it is important that cultural and rhetorical theory continue to include race theory and theories of difference in its critical vocabulary. Continuing to focus on race theory is important especially given that one of the unfortunate results of affirmative action policies, for example, is that the premise of such policies has become fuel for the advocating of a color-blind social policy by its enemies. The enemies of affirmative action argue that achievement should be based not on "preference" but on the result of individual effort only because racial discrimination is largely a thing of the past.

To "trade in old ideas" is to identify how the ideas in which we often "trade"—in the academy, in popular media—about identity and cultural difference are still largely based on racial thinking, on eighteenth and nineteenth century "ideologies of difference." It is also to suggest that to counter the oppressive logics of such racial thinking we need to "trade in" or displace them, as Frankenberg suggests, and replace these logics with kinds of thinking about cultural difference that are less reductive, less exploitative, and less monologically determined. Furthermore, seeing race as a changing and flexible "ideology of difference" is central to contemporary critical thought on difference and writing, precisely because writing is a matter of inscribing the world with meaning. Although we cannot "get outside of race," so to speak, we can work to revalue or, as Brodkey says, "transvalue" difference more complexly and positively in order to live with our differences and struggle for the right to be variously, not dualistically, different.

Audre Lorde writes that we have "*all* been programmed to respond to human differences between us with fear and loathing and to handle that difference" by either "ignoring it," "copying it," or "destroying it" (115). What we need to do, as Lorde points out, is to "relearn" *difference*, what it means to be different, and to struggle for the "right" to be critically, creatively, and variously different. Relearning and rewriting what it means to be different must also include rigorous analyses of the interlocking dimensions of race and gender as well as those of other axes of cultural positioning such as sexuality and nationality. But we cannot relearn and rewrite difference by remaining historically amnesic, by ignoring histories and policies of "othering" people, or by relying on outmoded and congealed ideas of cultural difference. What is crucial is learning how to teach, how to write about, how to argue for, how to negotiate critically our differences in ways that do not avoid the differences that matter: those of social, political, and economic inequality.

# Chapter Three

## Men's Studies, Feminism(s), and Rhetorics of Difference

> No subject is its own point of departure; and the fantasy that it is one can only disavow its constitutive relations by recasting them as the domain of a countervailing externality.
>
> —Judith Butler

> We need to think about what forms genuine political solidarity between men and women should take in a movement aimed at the liberation of women.
>
> —Sandra Bartky

If we accept, at least hesitantly, that critical analysis of the cultural signification of whiteness by whites is crucial in advancing anti-racist projects, then we might also consider how the critical analysis of the connections between male subjectivities and gender oppression by men can advance anti-sexist projects. A common response, however, to the emergence of what has come to be called men's studies is that such studies are merely more of the same: "Haven't we been focusing on men for thousands of years? After more than two thousand years of concentrating on men and their concerns, the last thing we need is men's studies." Such a response is understandable, because what "men's studies" signifies is neither evident nor coherent. Like feminism, men's studies is not monological but rather diverse, with differing and sometimes competing approaches toward issues surrounding gender and sexuality. Also, there are real stakes involved in men's formally entering the study of gender and sexuality, and, for this reason, it is important that claims on all sides be considered critically. Still, the answer to the above question is yes, we have been focusing on men and their concerns all this time; but, until the emergence of feminism, this had not been done in any explicitly coherent or critical manner, and men historically have not interrogated the connections between male subjectivities and gender oppression. In this chapter I want to make a case for critical men's studies' contribution to battling gender discrimination, something that cannot be done, I further argue, without engaging feminism(s) in a kind of critical negotiation.

Paraphrasing David Morgan, Harry Brod puts the situation of historically concentrating on men and their concerns in a non-critical manner this way: "While women have been obscured from our vision by being too much in the background, men have been obscured by being too much in the foreground" (40–41). And, as Adrienne Rich sees it, we have come to realize that objectivity has been little more than male subjectivity (3). Echoing Rich, Lad Tobin says that for "too many of those two thousand years, too many male scholars acted as if their studies were gender-neutral, implying that what they discovered in their research about men applied to women as well" (167). Although the lenses through which we have understood ourselves and the world have been primarily *man*-made, it wasn't until the advent of feminism, especially in its more recent stages, that androcentric ways of understanding and patriarchal social structures have come to be challenged and resisted in any kind of formidable way. Scholars in men's studies and feminism think that we are now to a point where the critical study of men and masculinity must be undertaken by men themselves in order to more fully challenge the longstanding, destructive effects of patriarchy and hegemonic masculinity, an assemblage of gender codes that defines how men are supposed to act, think, and feel if they are to be considered "real" men.

It is important to realize here that gender scripts for men, just as those for women, are not natural and universal; they do not transcend (exist before and beyond) the social and the historical. As R. W. Connell succinctly puts it: "If gender is a historical product, then it is open to historical change; this is what gender politics are about" (140). What it means to be a man, what it means to act like a man, typically explained in universal terms—those definitions that have so long been the reserves of the power of men over women—are to be resisted and redefined if we are to effectively counter gender oppression. The task for those involved in critical men's studies is not to argue for a renewed understanding of things through men's eyes but to initiate and sustain projects that interrogate the social construction of hegemonic masculinity and male subjectivities and how these constructions are connected to gender and sexual domination. As I see it, part of the objective is to counter such domination by positing a range of alternative male subjectivities that are not restricted wholly by hegemonic masculinity, subjectivities that are not built upon the domination of women.

Cases for men's studies and masculinity studies need to be explicitly stated, and men need to articulate clearly their positions on gender issues. Otherwise, as history bears out, men's positions become murky and invisible to scrutiny, derhetoricized and depoliticized. Jeff Hearn and David L. Collinson write, "there is a danger in focusing on men and masculinities, even within critical work, in a way that *reexcludes* women and 'femininities.' One way that avoids this possibility is to consistently locate men and masculinities as power relations" (98). Locating men and masculinities as/in power relations involves in part investigating how men are already situated and continue to situate themselves in relation to feminist interpretations of gender and sexuality. Not only are men situated by feminist interpretations, feminism too is immersed, as Elizabeth Grosz says, in patriarchal practices, "including those surrounding the production of theory." Realizing this immersion rather than disavowing it, Grosz argues, "is the condition of feminism's *emersion*, its effective critique of and movement beyond these practices" (95). What I am saying is that it is important to understand arguments for men's studies as resulting in part from the intertwined politics of patriarchy and feminist movement. Remaining alert to this imbrication can help men to resist reinscribing patriarchal codes as they argue for a better understanding of the operations of hegemonic masculinity and as they interrogate and resist their points of complicity in gender domination.

Clearly, cases for studying the construction of masculinity as a way to better understand the connections among gender domination, rhetoric, culture, and pedagogy must be explicitly articulated. But it is also important to realize that because of the deep and pervasive interconnectedness of the genders, separatist politics are not a realistic long-term option—although there are some who think they are. Only by forwarding the study of men and masculinity in relation to positions in feminism and queer theory, a critical negotiation, can inquiry into the connections among male subjectivities, rhetoric, and learning be for-

warded without forestalling the engagement crucial for multi-determinant forms of knowledge about gender and sexuality.

## Uneasy Engagements: Men and Feminism

Some scholars in men's studies have been discussing the need for men to
critique the constructed nature of their own subjectivities as well as the
need to rethink "masculine" identities. The objective is to begin to re-
create identities different from traditional ones that have been and are
often socialized to be alienated from emotional life and obsessed with
falsely objectified forms of knowledge. In order to rethink and re-create
"masculine" identities, it is important, as Brod writes, to study "masculinities and male experiences as specific and varying social-historical-
cultural formations" (40). That is, masculinity is constructed differently
by intersections of various other social axes—nationality, class, race, age,
for example—each of which modifies the others. Without understanding
this we risk collapsing all masculinities into one monologic version.

Furthermore, as Eve Kosofsky Sedgwick observes, "When something is about masculinity, it is not always 'about men.' It is important to
drive a wedge in, early and often and if possible conclusively, between the
two topics, masculinity and men, whose relation to one another it is so
difficult as not to presume" (12). Homi Bhabha writes that when studying
masculinity the aim should not be "to deny or disavow masculinity, but
to disturb its manifest destiny—to draw attention to it as a prosthetic
reality—a 'pre-fixing' of the rules of gender and sexuality" ("Are" 57–
58). But to argue for the complexity of masculine subjectivities, the
complexity of the concept of masculinity itself, and against the
overgeneralized claim that "all men oppress all women," does not weaken
feminist causes, nor does it discount the fact that patriarchy is cross-
culturally instituted; rather, such argumentation allows for nuancing strict
oppositional thinking (us versus them) and, in turn, allows for better
understanding of the multitudinous forms of male domination and of the
complex constitution of male subjectivities.

Inquiries into the complexity of masculinity are important aspects of
critical men's studies, and several feminist scholars have weighed in on
the debate about men's studies and men engaging in feminism. For
example, in a speech at the University of South Florida in March 1998,
third-wave feminist theorist and activist Rebecca Walker suggested,
among other things, that women's studies departments might begin

making institutional room for the critical study of men and masculinity in the form of men's studies courses so that the deleterious effects of hegemonic masculinity can be better understood, critiqued, and resisted. Sandra Harding has also argued for the need for men committed to feminism to "speak specifically as men, of themselves, of their bodies and lives, of texts and of politics, using feminist insights to see the world" (ix; qtd. in May et al.). Also, in an interview with Elizabeth Hirsh and Gary A. Olson, Harding says that men have "important, unusual, distinctive contributions of their own to make to feminism and to everybody's understanding of gender and social relations between the genders" (219). And Donna Haraway plainly states in an interview with Olson that

> Men have particular, actual, special, historical responsibilities about sexual violence and about the construction of a masculine gender position as aggressive—no question about that in my mind. That's one thing. Men also have an obligation to teach each other and to work with women for feminist projects and not to think that it's somebody else's responsibility—even in the face of many women who don't want men anywhere near. (19)

Haraway touches upon something I have talked about elsewhere when studying race: that those systematically discriminated against should not be expected to work out entirely on their own the problems that face them.[1]

Sandra Bartky puts the matter of pro-feminist men working in feminism this way:

> What I believe to be true of anti-racist whites (I include myself), I believe to be true of many men. There are men who do not want to be oppressors any longer: they too are repelled by a system that, unbidden, has bestowed privileges upon them which they have not earned, and which it denies to women. They do not want to be complicit in the subordination of half of humanity. They do not always succeed: just as a political stand against racism does not automatically free whites from some forms of racism, so the decision to struggle against sexism does not automatically extinguish in men a lifetime of sexist conditioning. ("Foreword" xiii)

Such ethical stances work from the realization that we all have a responsibility in countering oppressive social structures, structures in which we are all caught up, albeit in differing ways. But working *with* others is different from speaking *for* them, as Linda Alcoff has convincingly argued in "The Problem of Speaking for Others." Still, as Harding notes, dominant groups often think they know better, what's best for the oppressed, even when they are claiming to be working with them (Olson 219). Such paternalism stemming from privilege clearly needs to be avoided. Assuming that one knows what is best for someone else (How can we forget the television show *Father Knows Best*?) is a result of privilege; it is an idea, in fact, that stems from confusing privilege with knowledge. That is, having privilege over and against some group can very well lead one to act paternalistically, to believe one knows what is best for those seen as less fortunate or less privileged. Acting paternalistically from a position of privilege is clearly not the same as listening to and working with people toward realizing their needs and interests. That is why it is crucial to listen, to not impose, and to remember that those associated with dominant groups—whites and men, for example—must do their own difficult and critical work to resist racism and sexism. Those associated with dominant groups simply cannot expect to be educated by the "authentic" other in how to do this. Nor, as Laura Micciche points out, should feminism be expected to welcome men easily into the debate on gender and sexuality, or into institutional spaces such as women's studies departments for that matter. Such an expectation, she argues, is the "unsavory result of historical privilege granted men in a patriarchal culture. These privileges include open access to the world too often denied women, people of color, gays, and other 'deviants' from (white) male economy" (34).

The arguments of feminists such as Walker, Harding, Haraway, Bartky, and others for the critical study of men and masculinity signal a growing awareness that a strict oppositional stance along gender lines against male domination may not be enough to counter its debilitating effects. A strict oppositional stance along gender lines in this sense can also restrict creative resistance as well as block analysis of more insidious and subtle forms of domination that men, because of their socialization into traditional male roles, can address, undoubtedly contradictorily, from perspectives unique to themselves. In short, men must begin to know themselves and understand the effects of masculinity critically; and they must begin to act from there. Bell hooks writes that since "men are the primary agents maintaining and supporting sexism and sexist oppression, they can only be successfully eradicated if men are compelled to assume responsibility for transforming their consciousness and the consciousness of society as a whole" (*Feminist* 81). Bartky comments that the overgeneralized claim so popular in feminism's second wave that "all men oppress all women" must be rethought in times when it is necessary for new social movements to make strategic alliances among one another to combat the formidable forces of regressive and monologic gender politics. Part of such a project includes rethinking, she says, men's roles in feminism:

> For many men, the pain inflicted by the imposition of male gender identity serves as an entirely comprehensible motive for their active support in the women's movement. There is also at play here a matter of simple justice: many men have integrated feminist values and a profound commitment to the feminist movement into their lives, their personal relationships with both men and women, their relationships with children, their romantic involvements, their work, and, if they are academics, their research and teaching. These men deserve a place at our table: they have listened and learned from us; there is much we can learn from them. There are also practical reasons for abandoning a thoroughly separatist politics. Given the antiquity, power, depth and breadth of patriarchy, I doubt that women alone can overthrow it. We need "gender traitors," and lots of them, to effect a thoroughgoing reform of our institutions and a wholesale movement to a new plateau of consciousness. ("Foreword" xii)

This is not to discount, as Bartky continues, the belief that a movement for the liberation of women "should be led by women and answerable to them" nor to dismiss the argument that because of the emotionally, physically, and psychically damaging effects of patriarchy many women "want and need their own spaces and places." Lesbian separatists, for instance, "have invented news ways for women to be together, both socially and sexually; they have also made indispensable contributions to feminist theory" ("Foreword" xi-xii).[2] It is, however, to propose that by working together—not harmoniously, not coherently (How could this be possible without some violent force of assimilation?)—women and men can perhaps better dismantle not only the ossified remains of patriarchal ideology but resist as well contemporary regressive politics that seek to merge with and reenergize such ideology. Bartky also points out that some men are more committed to feminism and ending sexism than some women, a realization, however, that does not discount that these very same women often feel the negative effects of patriarchy and sexism whereas their pro-feminist male counterparts do not.

As many scholars both in men's studies and feminism point out, it is crucial that the interrogation of men and masculinity be carried on *in relation to* feminist positions. It is crucial to remember this and act from it. Thinking that the critical study of men and masculinity could be undertaken as if feminism never existed, as if what men think of themselves has been constructed only by men, as if men have been hermetically sealed off from women's interpretations, is all symptomatic of an approach to gender that necessitates the articulation of feminism in the first place. Such is the case with the Mythopoetic Men's Movement, for example, a movement comprised of groups of white, middle-aged, heterosexual, and largely professional men who see a need for men "to retreat from women to create spiritually based homosocial rituals through which they can collectively recapture a lost or strayed 'true manhood'" (Messner 17). The irony missed here is that "these organized attempts to grapple with the meanings of masculinity by retreating from women would not exist if feminism had not raised 'the man question' in the first place" (Messner 16). Men need to think of creative, nonreductive ways that positions in men's studies can be put into dialogue with feminist positions in order to better understand gender relations, respect gender and sexual differences, and counter sexism. Many involved in critical men's studies, for example, have admitted an indebtedness to feminism and women's studies. I don't feel this is merely a polite, formal gesture. Many men, for example, argue their positions in relation to feminist ones. Admitting indebtedness to feminism is not so much about respect as it is about reality; these men would be incapable of working the theoretical ground they are now working if it were not for the contributions of feminists and feminism.

Nevertheless, pro-feminist men often find engaging in male feminism difficult because, as hooks notes, their politics are often disdained by anti-feminist men and women (*Feminist* 79). Also, they are sometimes ignored by some feminists or worse charged with careerism and opportunism. Bartky writes, however, that few men benefit from too close an alliance with feminism, that such alliances tend more to discredit a man than advance his career: "Coming out for feminism regularly earns a man not only the distrust of many feminist women, but the scorn of 'manly' men, who charge him of having been 'pussywhipped'" ("Foreword" xiii). But this is not to make a special plea on men's behalf: be kind to men in feminism, let them in without conflict, understand them. Such a sentiment can be understood as resulting from male privilege. (Although recognizing men's achievements in this area is not an entirely abhorrent sentiment.) Rather, I want to encourage men to meet what Cornel West refers to as the existential challenge of doing critical work: the ability to generate and sustain "the self-confidence, discipline, and perseverance necessary for success without undue reliance on the mainstream for approval and acceptance" (25). I must stress here that in order to meet such a challenge it is imperative that men listen for awhile, without imposition, to the many theorists and activists who have been working against compulsory heterosexist, patriarchal, and racist ideological structures long before (straight?) (white?) men ever thought of doing so in any coherent manner. It would be helpful too if we thought of pro-feminist men not as opportunists but rather as committed scholars seeking to advance the critical study of men's subjectivities *and* an end to gender domination, the difficulties of which are obviously inevitable and unavoidable. Commitment comes not from men avoiding difficulty (the "distrust of many feminist women") or dodging ridicule (the "scorn of 'manly' men") but from redoubling their efforts to argue self-critically, passionately, and cogently from the intersections of their own perspectives and those of feminist scholars. It should be clear that men's studies and the critical study of masculinity are inevitable outgrowths of feminism and that men's studies would not be possible at this historic moment without feminism. They are inevitable outgrowths of feminism not only because men, both progressive and conservative, have felt the need to elaborate on and respond to feminism respectively, but also because feminism has given us critical methods and vocabularies from a variety of perspectives to study sex and gender relations as well as the complicated, cross-cultural functioning of patriarchal domination.

What Bartky calls "gender traitors," pro-feminist men, should be coming to seem more and more like allies in the fight against women's oppression, especially in the face of the kinds of regressive masculinism represented, for example, by those men of the Nation of Islam and the Promise Keepers. On gender issues, such factions are reactionary because they blame feminism for a host of social maladies, and they are regressive because they advocate men's reaffirming rather than questioning traditional male roles. Such factions also reinforce forms of *hegemonic masculinity* rather than critique them, thereby foreclosing attempts to rearticulate less oppressive alternatives. If we accept, at least tenuously, the need for pro-feminist men to ally with feminist women in the fight against sexism, a central project then becomes theorizing an *ethics of engagement* through which we can productively engage our differences as men and women in order to better counter gender discrimination.

## Impossible Relations, Objective Inadequacies

What, then, is a productive guideline for thinking of the engagement among the various positions in feminism, masculinity studies, and queer theories? In Chapter 1, I discussed *critical negotiation*, a way of thinking about negotiation less as a mere dealing and more as a dialogic process or ethics of engagement that takes into account the role of emotion as well as the operations of various social axes of positioning in social and political interaction. I think the concept is appropriate in this case, and it might be helpful to begin by posing problems and asking questions that are intended to produce thinking about gendered subjectivities that is materially-grounded, relational, critical, complex, and varied. Working from ideas put forward by Stephen Heath, I want to propose that the relations among the positions in the study of gender and sexuality are ones that are imaginable but not achievable in any kind of final and lasting sense. Micciche says that men cannot have an easy relation to feminism, that they must work to achieve a critical relation to it (33). In men's achieving critical relations to feminism, it might be helpful to consider Heath's idea that "men's relation to feminism is an impossible one," that all feminist positions begin with the premise that "*his* experience is *her* oppression" (1, 2; emphasis added). The (critical) negotiation by women between their experiences and feminist interpretations is, according to Heath, what feminist theory is fundamentally about. Since "*his* experience is *her* oppression," men are blocked *objectively* in such a negotiation; they must, however, confront or engage this starting point of feminism, the very basis of feminism: not how "all men oppress all women," but where, how, and why they are complicit in structures of patriarchal domination and hegemonic masculinity. If men do not do this, they deny the very project of feminism and imagine to their satisfaction "a possible relation instead of the difficult, contradictory, self-critical, painful, impossible one that men must, for now, really live" (Heath 2).

Lynn Worsham has urged men to seek a relation to feminism in which they learn to respect boundaries and to consider what she calls the "objective inadequacy" of "male feminism":

> There are objective limits to what men can know—objective limits
> to the access they can have to the position of women and to an
> understanding of themselves—precisely because they are not born
> and made female-sexed subjects in a racist patriarchy. Their

contributions to knowledge will remain, until that symbolic economy is overthrown, merely theoretical. Men must struggle to achieve a relation to feminism as anti-sexist collaborators and to reconstruct masculinity for themselves. ("Romancing" 570)

Heath's notion of an "impossible relation" and Worsham's idea of "objective inadequacy" are not meant to discourage men from engaging in projects of self-critique and initiating dialogue with feminist positions; rather, they are meant to alert pro-feminist men to the difficulty of the task ahead of them and to argue for the need to respect and interrogate the *objective* differences between men and women. Objective differences are those differences lived through material conditions and in social life—wage inequities based on gender, the pervasiveness of sexual harassment and rape, for example. Objectively, men cannot experience life under patriarchy as women do, and any attempt by men to speak *for* women in this sense can only be seen as a move to disempower women by discounting their experiences, interpretations, and voices. However, because feminism is a theoretical and political stance and not something that automatically comes with being a woman, men can work *with* women to counter the harmful effects of patriarchy and sexism; they can be involved in feminism. Men can do *kinds* of feminism; they can be, as Worsham says, "collaborators." But the work they do is different from that of women; it is not feminism *as such*, but perhaps, as Heath suggests, *male feminism*.

Thinking about *critical engagement* in this context as the kind of "impossible relation" that Heath suggests represents a commitment to forestall closed-ended interpretations of human subjectivity based on gender and sexuality. It also means acting from the realization that our differences are objective *and* personal, that they are material *and* rhetorical. Because our differences are "real" and cannot simply be papered over or ignored; fostering intersubjective ways of "understanding" is crucial. This includes those forms of feeling and thinking that allow people to make connections across political and ideological borders, connections motivated by strong political emotion: empathy for the suffering of others, yearning for social justice, and anger in the face of the chauvinism and elitism that compromise people's lives and options. The fundamental importance of the emotions to social and political life is one reason that men's cultivating a more open, easy, and deeper connection to their emotional lives and the emotional lives of others is a key to transformational gender politics. Being committed to difference while acting from common passions implies a dedication to work together self-critically to counter sexual and gender oppression. Also, a commitment to such engagement doesn't mean that this will be an easy ride or that working together does not entail, at times, working against one another. We occupy different positions and have different needs, the arguments from and for which may at times intersect chiasmus-like, only to diverge as our differences take us elsewhere. Ultimately, we want our politics to cross paths and separate because our various trajectories should be leading us in different ways in the same general direction: a less oppressive society based on gender divisions.

## Learning and the Rituals of Gender

My argument so far has been for scholars in men's studies to engage positions in feminism in ways that respect the terms and boundaries of these positions as well as the discourses of feminism. I have argued that it is important that men not demonize or discount feminism, or simply blame feminism for men's problems. And I have posited an ethics of engagement, or critical negotiation, wherein supporting reductionistic interpretations of gendered subjectivities is anathema to the kind of thinking needed to make necessary theoretical claims beyond our gendered "borders." Now I want to turn attention to gender and pedagogy—more specifically, to the connection between learning and the rituals or performances of gender. What I want to take up here specifically is the charge by Robert J. Connors that the pervasiveness of feminist modes of teaching—collaboration and group work, for example—has hindered male students' ability to learn because men typically are socialized toward competitive individualism rather than toward cooperation. In his article, "Teaching and Learning as a Man," Connors does not engage feminism but seems content to blame feminism—particularly models of collaboration and group work associated with feminist ways of teaching—for the learning problems of young men. Not only does he see the learning problems of young men as a direct result of the success of feminist ways of teaching, he also sees these problems as stemming in part from the disappearance of masculinity rituals from contemporary cultures—those rituals that initiate boys into manhood. I argue, however, that such rituals have not disappeared, but that they have merely taken less spectacular and more secular forms, forms alive and well as gender scripts and gender performances.[3]

Working from Walter Ong's *Fighting for Life*, Connors argues that the agonistic dimensions of rhetoric and teaching became emasculated by the entrance of women into the academy, giving rise to composition-rhetoric, which is "internalized rather than public, multimodal rather than purely argumentative" (142). Men had to tone down the verbal aggressiveness of rhetorical agonism—the "constant struggle for power, physical comfort, ego-satisfaction, territory"—because of the entrance of women into higher education (140). However, because of the success of feminist ways of teaching—emphasis on collaboration and group work—many young men have come to feel alienated and uncomfortable in today's learning environments and, consequently, are unsure how to act in them, according to Connors. He asks that we seek to understand that because men are socialized toward aggressive individualism they will consistently disappoint if "egalitarian, communitarian, consensus-based collaboration is part of a teacher's expectations of group work" (154). Certainly it is important for teachers to attempt to understand how young men are socialized to be solitary, aggressive, and competitive, and how this affects learning; it is important that we do not simply dismiss young men's attitudes in learning situations as inherently defiant, aloof, or hostile. It is also necessary to better understand that how male and female students are socialized into traditional gender roles influences how they react to different learning styles and environments. I also agree with Connors that "expecting that we can blunt the aggressive individualism that *is* men's cultural training in a few weeks is unrealistic" (145).

But Connors does not go far enough here; he only wants us to understand young men's confusion and pain in order to help them through it. He does not shed light on how we can interrogate and resist the structures of hegemonic masculinity that provide restrictive gender scripts for men, nor does he offer ways to interrogate and rearticulate traditional masculine subjectivities. More than this, he seems rather content simply to blame feminism for the learning problems of young men. Ultimately, what Connors ends up doing is calling for male teachers to act in therapeutic capacities toward their male students. He also is not concerned with interrogating masculinity rituals, only with lamenting how, because of the disappearance of these rituals, young men are getting cues about what it means to be a man from elsewhere—the media and peer groups, for example.

By focusing on mentoring male students as they negotiate the confusing learning environment brought about by feminist teaching methods, Connors advocates something very similar to what Connell refers to as

"masculinity therapy" found in mythopoetic factions of the men's movement. Connell writes that masculinity therapy

> is a psychological "recovery" movement, addressed to hetero-
> sexual men's pain and uncertainties about gender. At the base of
> this politics is the complicit masculinity that accepts the broad
> structure of gender relations but is not militant in its defense. The
> clients of masculinity therapists are mostly white and middle class,
> and often middle aged. They feel they are in trouble, and they feel
> they are unfairly blamed by feminists. Some of their theories, in
> fact, claim that men are more disadvantaged than women. All of
> them say it is men's turn for the kind of attention feminism has
> been gaining for the problems of women. (146)

There is nothing wrong with wanting psychically and emotionally healthier
and more well-adjusted male students. In fact, many men's studies
scholars think that men's cultivating a more open and deeper connection to their emotional lives and the emotional lives of others is a key
"to the transformation of personal relationships, sexuality, and domestic life" (Connell 136). However, the problem with the masculinity therapy model advocated by Connors and mythopoetic factions lies
with the acceptance of gender structures as they are and with the
blaming of feminism for men's problems. Those of the mythopoetic
movement do not attack the hegemonic gender scripts that both restrict
men's lives and encourage gender discrimination but, in fact, do just
the opposite: they seek to reaffirm traditional identities of men and
their roles in society. Like others of this movement, Connors sees the
reinstatement of masculinity rituals as a kind of male therapy, as a way to
put young men "back on track" so that they know truly how and when to
consider themselves "men." To complete the implicit argument: This
process would go a long way toward putting the rest of society back on
track.

Connors' emphasis on ritualized masculinity, Micciche observes,
provokes a basic question: Why do men need social rituals or initiation
ceremonies in order to feel "like men"?:

> A patriarchal culture hard-pressed to maintain gender socializa-
> tion, to distinguish "men" from "boys," has much investment in
> this need to ritualize the arrival "into" manhood. But rather than
> simply creating social rituals that fulfill patriarchy's need to code
> bodies, an examination of masculinity as a goal to be attained

benefits men *and* women, men's studies *and* feminism. It is also a more humane and politically responsible alternative than merely satisfying the brutality of the status quo. (34)

Connors' conservative position on masculinity rituals is one that argues for the reinstatement of rituals that code bodies so that boys will know how to act properly as men, so that they will not only know their "proper" place in society, but that of women as well. As Micciche points out, an examination rather than an uncritical acceptance of the need to attain manhood can work to counter gender domination rather than perpetuate it.

I think too that Connors has forwarded a rather unnuanced understanding of collaboration and has too simply linked collaboration and group work in the classroom to the expressed objectives of *some feminists*. Susan C. Jarratt, for example, has pointed out how feminism is linked often uncomplicatedly and inaccurately to pedagogies that seek to avoid conflict and confrontation. Also, in "Collaboration, Conversation, and the Politics of Gender," Evelyn Ashton-Jones convincingly argues that the ideology of gender often is reproduced in the interactional dynamics of group work in the classroom (7). Complicating things further, she observes that feminist valorization of collaborative learning often discourages analysis and unwittingly leads to collusion in the reproduction of gender structures that feminists seek to disrupt (7).

As a kind of classroom ritual, collaboration often reinforces and reproduces traditional gender roles and, for this reason, does not always alienate male students. While some male students work well and cooperatively in these situations, I have seen male students not respond to group work (as Connors describes observing) thereby disappointing my expectations. But I have also seen them dominate and take control of things as well, a situation Connors mentions observing only in all-male groups (154). By limiting his observations to male students dominating only in all-male groups, Connors conveniently avoids dealing with the fact that some male students work very well in mixed groups through imposition and assertion, by taking on traditional male roles. In these situations, men are not alienated at all, but reinforced in their competitive and assertive roles.

I wonder, however, if some male students who don't work well in groups are not those who feel alienated by feminist modes of teaching but are those who may be struggling with and attempting to resist restrictive gender scripts. Uncomfortable with traditional roles of assertive leadership, they may be unsure how to act and, thus, take themselves out of the game. Connors thinks, I think unwisely, that all male students are wrestling with becoming men in traditional senses. Certainly, as he points out, "college years present young people with their most complex challenges of self-definition" (146). But his research is limited by his inability to imagine a broad range of male subjectivities; he does not explore the possibility that some male students may be struggling with how *not* to become men in traditional senses, that they might be struggling *against* restrictive scripts of assertion and competition. For this reason, the learning problems of young men should not be handled by coddling them as they negotiate these formative times. It might be better instead to examine the social and political ramifications of such formative times, to study and discuss how men's and women's identities proceed from a series of avowals and disavowals, investments in an economy of gender that configure relations in gendered terms.

But how do "boys" or "guys"—an age-neutral and even mostly gender-neutral term, as Connors accurately observes—construct themselves as men? Connors notes that cultural forms that in the past have indicated a boy's passage into manhood—rites and rituals of passage—have pretty much disappeared. Looking at the surface of things, this is a fairly accurate observation. However, I do not think that such rituals that let boys know that they're men are things of the past. I think that they have merely taken other less spectacular, less ritualized, and more secular forms.

Part of the project of critical men's studies today is to interrogate the making of masculinities and "men," and this includes studying masculinity rituals and performances of gender. But such study should not chronicle and lament the passing of such rituals but interrogate not only their social functioning but also how explicit rituals of gender socialization are coming to be re-formed into implicit ones. Part of this task is to identify how repetitive performances of masculinity operate visibly and invisibly so as to instruct boys in how they are to act as men. Certain performances of masculinity may be acting as rituals, as operations of gender ideology, without our viewing them as rituals *per se*. We might consider these performances of gender to be what I call *tacit rituals*, those recurring and repetitive performances that tell people who they are as men, as women, as racialized subjects, as classed subjects, as children, and so on. These kinds of rituals are repetitive performances of gender that serve in conservative capacities to reinforce traditional gender roles. Such rituals are different from the kinds of explicit and often parodic gender performances of masculinity and femininity—such as drag for instance—that can act, as Judith Butler has argued, in transgressive ways to deconstruct the binary structure of dominant ideologies of gender. Although tacit rituals function in social capacities similarly to more traditional rituals, they often are not seen to. Rituals do not need to be *ritualized*—that is, explicit and ceremonial. A ritual can be any practice or behavior *affected by accretion*, a practice or behavior that gains meaning by being repeated in a prescribed manner. Rituals and rites of passage in older senses had to be explicit in order to demonstrate to both initiates and observers that the initiated had "arrived" and crossed "the threshold" into a new stage of life. But with the loss of these explicit rituals, we get implicit ones; that is, they do not simply disappear but are re-formed. If it were the case that rituals of gender, for example, had disappeared, we would be living in a totally new and different society rather than in one that has merely put fresh spins on old structures.

Connors is accurate when he says that men look to peer groups and macho movies, for example, for role models. And he is right that we need to be aware of and critique the effects of such films and groups on shaping the consciousness of young men. But engaging in peer group activity and watching macho movies are ritualistic acts *in themselves*; that is, subjectivity is shaped in part not only through the content or message of cultural texts but through the very acts of consuming them, individually and collectively. These acts—reception and consumption—themselves become ritualistic in effect and function; they become patterned performances of gender socialization and identification based on shared experience. We need only to watch some all-male groups socializing in order to see certain "ceremonial" performances of manhood: whooping, high-fiving, excessive drinking, the telling of sexist jokes, referring to women degradingly, and so on. Such performances of masculinity differ depending on social axes such as profession and age, while some similarities cut across many axes. Beer ads are certainly getting quite a bit of mileage from (stereo)typical portrayals of men in homosocial interaction as groups of beer-swilling, sports-addicted, insensitive, childish boors.

But rituals of gender performance and identification are also at work in mixed settings. For example, Linda Alcoff refers to inequitable gendered patterns of interaction as "rituals of speaking," "discursive practices of speaking or writing that involve not only the text or utterance but also their position within a social space that includes the persons

involved in, acting upon, and/or affected by words" ("Problem" 102).
Regarding gender, she continues,

> When a woman speaks the presumption is against her; when a man
> speaks he is usually taken seriously (unless his speech patterns
> mark him as socially inferior by dominant standards). The rituals
> of speaking, which involve the locations of speaker and listeners,
> affect whether a claim is taken as a true, well-reasoned, compelling
> argument or significant idea. Thus, how what is said gets heard
> depends on who says it and who says it will affect the style and
> language in which it is stated. (103)

Ashton-Jones also observes that women's claims are often devalued not
necessarily because of their content but because of women's social
positioning *as women*. She notes that the speaking rituals of gender during
conversation involve the accepted interruption or "talking over" of
women by men, as well as the expectation that women will do most of the
connective or "support work" in conversations—starting and facilitating
conversations, for example. We often think of the interruption of women
by men as simply rude, but such an interpretation prevents us from seeing
that these gendered conversational dynamics are more about systematic
operations of gender ideology and less about rules of politeness or
manners. Interruptions, for instance, can be interpreted as "power plays
that not only reflect gender hierarchy but serve as 'reminders' to women
of their second class status" (Ashton-Jones 15). These kinds of conversational dynamics, I argue, can be seen as gender rituals: ones that let men
and women know their positions in the order of things. These dynamics
are often so normalized and accepted as to seem invisible. For this reason,
they are good examples of what I am calling *tacit rituals*.

Repetitive *performances of manhood* in part tell boys how they
should act in order to be thought of as men; they let them know early in
life their social positions in relation to women. These performances may
be seen as *tacit rituals*—tacit because they are not explicit like traditional
ones—but rituals nonetheless because they help socialize boys into
manhood and tell men who they are and how to act in relation to women.
Thinking of gender socialization in this way, one is tempted to revise the
Althussarian idea of interpellation—the address of culture or the subject-
forming work of ideology. It should be clear, however, that the language
work we do in rhetoric and cultural studies is important to the continuing
examination of the role that rhetoric plays in gender performance and the
formation of gender consciousness.

## Sexuality and the Queering of Gender

It is interesting that in all Connors' talk of men and masculinity, in his argument to "confront gender issues wholly," his rhetoric, concerns, preoccupations, and arguments primarily center on "unmarked" men: those who are white and heterosexual. Absent is any talk of how the axes of sexual orientation, class, and race, for example, intersect with and help to constitute male subjectivities in various ways. Also, Connors' idea of mentoring, his "masculine therapy" for young male students, seems to be available only to those who are white and middle class; those men of discriminated groups of all kinds, it appears, are out of luck. It's not that he need presume to make claims for all men, but if he truly is interested in the learning processes of *men*, then his avoidance of the interlocking dynamics of sexuality, class, and race is an unfortunate oversight. By leaving out the concerns and issues particular to gay men and men of color, Connors proposes that teaching and learning "as a man" is teaching and learning as a straight, white, largely middle-class man. If he is concerned with focusing on *men* and expanding emotional and subjective registers, he, in fact, does the opposite and helps to restrict such range. Focusing on how men teach and learn differently in relation to women and to one another should not simply be a project that focuses on how *some men* teach and learn.

If we are to focus on how *men* teach and learn rather than on what it is to teach and learn *as a man*, then it is important to realize also that some of our male students might not need help realigning themselves with hegemonic masculinity through manhood rituals; in fact, some may be attempting to distance themselves from the constructions of hegemonic masculinity. Queer theory, gay studies, and lesbian studies can help us think about rearticulating alternative masculine subjectivities over and against those posited by heterosexist and hegemonic paradigms by helping to show that masculinity is in part a performance and that masculinity, as Sedgwick says, is not always about men. Queer theory in particular can help us to think outside the dominant, binary logic of heterosexuality, which also undergirds ideas of homosexuality, thereby working to relax the compulsory grip of heterosexist normativity.

Sexuality, like emotion, traditionally has been deemed marginal to political life, sometimes by standards of rationality, propriety, morality, and/or reason, but primarily because sex is experienced subjectively and because it largely concerns the body. Increasingly over the past decades, sexuality has moved closer to politics due in large part to the efforts of those associated with gay and lesbian movements, which have sought to affirm gay and lesbian identities for community building and for political leverage.[4] However, saying that gay and lesbian movements often have similar general objectives—protection from homophobic discrimination, positive self-redefinition—is not to claim that there are not differences between and, in fact, within these movements. Some lesbian theorists, for example, have found it necessary both to focus on the interlocking structures of gender and sexual oppression and to emphasize that gay men do not automatically shed sexist notions and behaviors.

Although gay and lesbian movements have made great strides in affirming gay and lesbian identities for purposes of community building and political leverage, it is queer theory and politics that most strongly challenge gender as an ideology of difference. That is, gay theory and politics examine and challenge how the categories of both homo- and heterosexuality are based on the binary logic of heterosexist paradigms. Much queer theory begins with the premise that because "our existing theories of homosexuality and heterosexuality do a fair amount of violence to the human variety that they claim to describe" (A. Martin 325), it is necessary to interrogate and dismantle the constitution of these regimes of sexual difference so that we may then rearticulate sexual identities along less restrictive lines. Connell says that

> queer politics involves a reversal of the mainstream approach of gay politics, contesting and dismantling identities rather than affirming them as bases for community building. There is no doubt about the creativity of this movement and the rel- evance of its cultural critique to the dismantling of hegemonic masculinity. (147)

Because queer theory and politics are based on difference and sexuality, their transformative aim, as Nancy Fraser puts it, is not to "solidify a gay identity but to destabilize all fixed sexual identities." The point is not to dissolve all sexual difference into a postmodern orgy of omnisexuality; it is, rather, "to sustain a sexual field of multiple, debinarized, fluid, ever- shifting differences" (24). This does not leave us in a condition of *relative androgyny* in which sexual difference is erased and identities can be taken on and off or changed like shoes. Queer theory highlights, among other things, that sexuality and identity are in part performative (that the doer is invariably constructed in and through the deed) and that masculinity and femininity are not inherently and essentially associated with men and women respectively. Masculinity and femininity, according to Sedgwick, can be productively interpreted as "threshold effects": "places where quantitative increments along one dimension can suddenly appear as qualitative differences somewhere else on the map entirely" (16).

Much queer theory, and feminist theory as well, has helped to show that the categories of gender, homosexuality, and heterosexuality rely on the binary logic of dominant masculinist paradigms. Not only has the focus on the performative aspects of sexuality brought fresh insights to the workings of gender and sexual oppression, but also "antinormative queerness," writes Biddy Martin, "has become a welcome relief for those of us who have felt constrained, even obscured, by feminists' injunctions to identify with and as women, over against men and masculinity" (105). Despite all this, Martin warns, we must be careful not "to construct 'queerness' as a vanguard position that announces its newness and advance over against an apparently superseded and now anachronistic feminism with its emphasis on gender" (104). Although focusing on sexuality and affirming queerness can lead to more in depth interpretations of social identities, it would be unwise to dismiss gender as a category of the past, like some are dismissing race, "suitable now only for the dustbin of history" (Omi and Winant 55). To dismiss gender as an archaic category would mean that sexual difference is all there is, that the objective antecedents and correlatives of gender interpretations and politics do not make a difference. In short, it would involve an historical amnesia toward the constitution of gender difference. Nevertheless, *queering* is a powerful way to use sexuality as an analytical lens in order to expose the historical and material constructedness of gender categories and the constructed nature of heterosexual normativity, or what Adrienne Rich has called "compulsory heterosexuality."

Heterosexuality as ideologically compulsory can be seen as an effect of patriarchy that is as equally restrictive to men as it is to women. Gay studies, lesbian studies, and queer theory provide valuable and important critiques of hegemonic masculinity, and, as such, they provide ways to counter the damaging and restrictive effects of hegemonic masculinity as well as ways to articulate alternative subjectivities to those posited by the strict binary logic of gender. As long as we are careful not to let studies of gender performance and sexuality overshadow studies of the objective conditions of women, it would serve us well to be aware of the capability of queer theory to interrogate the operations of gender as an ideology of difference. Doing this might help us to rearticulate or rewrite male subjectivities as ones that see masculinity and femininity as "threshold effects," subjectivities that further do not idealize models of sexual difference based on hierarchy and dominance.

## Teaching and Learning *Like* Men: What's Next?

Connors' "as" in his title "Teaching and Learning as a Man" does not indicate a relationship among women and men, nor among men themselves for that matter. I want my revision of Connors' title to indicate that men teach and learn not in relation to some archetypal *man*, but like *men*— with various social positionings and relations to the world, to women, and to one another. The "like" in my heading I take from the talk of students; here it is meant to indicate hesitation and similarity, not immediacy and sameness.

Connors seems to agree with those of the mythopoetic men's movement who think that heterosexual white men need an identity politics of their own, one from which they are able not only argue their points coherently but one that offers therapy and consolation as well, one that seeks to understand their particular problems and how feminism has cast them in a bad light. Moreover, his stance tends to conflate feminisms into Feminism in order to lay blame rather than engage feminist positions on their own terms. Connors seems close to repeating the mistakes of early white, middle class feminists who advanced understandings of *woman* and of "women's rights" by excluding the insights and experiences of lesbians and women of color. What goes for women and feminism in this case goes for men and men's studies: "The minute that the category of women is invoked as *describing* the constituency for which feminism speaks, an internal debate invariably begins over what the descriptive content of the term will be" (Butler, "Contingent" 15).

Scholars interested in countering gender domination and advancing the critical study of men and masculinity do not need to step back, but ahead. We do not need regressive white male retrenchment, an identity politics based on backlash and blame, but progressive gender politics that recognize the need for alliance-building and coalition politics across lines of gender and sexual difference without erasing, avoiding, or ignoring the historical constitution or objective materialities of those differences. This is a form of what I have been calling critical negotiation. Bhabha thinks that it is important to know what claims white males in particular are making for themselves in the context of men's studies: "I would be as untrusting of a group that's actually pronouncing itself guilty as a group that's saying that everybody's trying to make them feel guilty and they don't feel guilty" ("Staging" 36). Men engaging in critical men's studies should not simply blame themselves for all problems relating to gender— a curious move but, more importantly, a politically ineffective one. But they should not seek to dodge points of complicity in structures of gender discrimination either; instead they should seek to initiate and sustain interrogations of the social construction of hegemonic masculinity and male subjectivities and further inquire into how these constructions are connected to gender and sexual discrimination.

In "Five Propositions on the Future of Men in Feminism," Jonathan Culler observes that men are positioned in relation to feminism in much the same way that they are positioned in relation to language or to history: "A man necessarily positions himself in relation to feminist thinking and writing of one sort or another, whether he quotes it, argues with it, ignores it, or seeks to carry it further" (187). In other words, because of the successes of feminism in the academy (although there is still much work to be done), a man doing any kind of gender work must necessarily not only consciously and deliberately position himself but must realize how he is *already positioned* in relation to feminism and feminist thinking. Even avoiding and ignoring feminism are deliberate acts, perilous as they are. Culler's observation has important implications for those men working with feminist ideas engaging in the critical study of men and masculinity. Such an observation points to the necessity that one must theorize from a socio-political location and that one is already situated in discourses of gender and sexual relations. Culler continues, saying that men in the academy "cannot choose whether to be in feminism or to keep out" (187). How men are to work *in relation to* feminism then becomes a central question for those men engaging in the critical study of men and masculinity.

Not only do men need to work to achieve a critical relation to feminism, they need to think of how the axes of sexual orientation, nationality, ethnicity, class, race, and age intersect with and help to construct masculinity in historically specific contexts. We don't need a kind of straight white men's movement, or the kind of men's identity politics that Connors forwards, ones that come perilously close to advancing the kind of uncritical celebration of essential masculinity that has been going on for over two thousand years. Lad Tobin, like Connors, argues that we need to pay more attention to the cultures of adolescent males. I agree. But Tobin talks of empathy rather than therapy, interrogation rather than consolation, which are much more effective ways, I think, to work with young men to understand their learning processes and to expand the range of emotional registers through which to interface with the world and others.

Michael Kimmel writes that "our fears are the sources of our silence, and men's silence is what keeps the system running" (131). The fears Kimmel speaks of are those of men publicly disavowing traditional notions of manhood by resisting the discriminatory logic of hegemonic masculinity. Kimmel sees men's silence and inaction based on fear and deep ambivalence about resisting hegemonic male codes and rituals. Because of investments in hegemonic masculinity, the men's club, many men fear the accusation: if you're not for us, you're against us. It would serve women and men well to foster an atmosphere wherein the political and ideological functioning of hegemonic masculinity is explicitly interrogated by men as well as by women, an atmosphere in which men are encouraged to disavow the restrictive codes of hegemonic masculinity and rearticulate male subjectivities along less oppressive lines. However, we must also realize that there are deep affective implications for such disavowal, because disavowal represents a shifting of power relations. A shifting politics of this sort creates within some men deep feelings of uneasiness, ambivalence, and fear, especially in those not accustomed to sharing power and desperate to retain privilege. For this reason, it is important to posit options for action other than oppositional reaction, actions more creative and critical than lashing back with dismissal, blame, and anger. It is also crucial, as I will discuss in the next chapter, to initiate sustained studies of the connections between rhetoric, emotion, and violence—or what we might call the affective politics of difference.

# Chapter Four

# Rhetoric, Emotion, and the Affective Violence of Difference

> We need a political phenomenology of the emotions—an examination of the role of emotion, most particularly of the emotions of self-assessment both in the constitution of subjectivity and in the perpetuation of subjection.
> —Sandra Lee Bartky

> The trenches dug within our hearts.
> —U2

While scholars of critical theory and critical pedagogy have had much to say about the multivalent and cross-cultural workings of ideology, they have had less to say about the interconnections between ideology and emotion. In large part, the role of strong emotions such as those of hate and anger, as well as violence, both real and symbolic, in processes of cultural differentiation and social discrimination remain undertheorized. Investigations into the relations among rhetoric, emotion, violence, and oppression are necessary to better engage the full affective range of discrimination and "othering" working along and across lines of nationality, sexuality, gender, and race. Studies that center on analyzing the affective relations of difference, I argue, must 1) look seriously at two of the more political emotions, those of anger and hatred, operating in today's politics of difference and engagement, and 2) theorize these in explicitly social, political, and pedagogical terms, not only in psychological and individual

71

ones. Rhetorical theorist Lynn Worsham has outlined what I think is a productive way to discuss these issues. She has outlined a rhetoric of "pedagogic violence" that seeks to describe "both the forms and effects through which violence is lived and experienced and its objective or structural role in the constitution of subjectivities and in the justification of subjection" ("Going" 215). Her objective is to examine "the way violence addresses and educates emotion and inculcates an affective relation to the world." It is further to expose what she sees as the occluded relationship between these pedagogical dimensions and "the bodily rhetoric of violence" as well as "its visible and invisible scarification of the individual and social psyche" ("Going" 215, 216). In this chapter, I want to trace Worsham's idea of "pedagogic violence" in order to inform my discussion of the difference between the pedagogical dimensions of a politics of anger and those of a politics of hate. I conclude by arguing that the politics and terms of any engagement cannot be understood fully without taking into account the intensely political and social dimensions of the affective relations of difference.

Studies in the ways in which violence and emotion influence our relations to ourselves, the world, and others are necessary if we are to advance a rhetorical politics that not only engage in the study of difference with our hearts as well as with our heads but that do not further entrench reason/emotion hierarchies. When studying the politics of engagement and difference we might consider rhetoric not only as the marshalling of *logos* but as the strategic display and restraint of emotions for social and political ends. Otherwise, sexist and racist notions toward emotion—the belief that women and racially marginalized groups, for example, are inherently more emotional—remain intact, devaluing the political effectivity of emotion and those closely associated with it. In short, articulating material-rhetorical theories and pedagogies that interrogate the emotion of politics and the politics of emotion are necessary if we are to better understand the role of emotion, especially anger and hatred, in matters of cultural difference.

## Worsham's "Pedagogic Violence"

Cultural differences involve more than just the ways in which we think about one another; they also involve the ways in which we feel about one another. Ways of feeling are not purely psychological and individual; they are structural and political as well. Consequently, we might say that emotions are educable, that they can be taught and learned. For these reasons, there is a real need to examine the complex relations among emotion, pedagogy, rhetoric, and violence, and how affective relations are imbricated with representations of cultural differences. In thinking about how emotions can be taught and learned—their pedagogic dimensions—it might be helpful to distinguish between two senses of pedagogy. The first, of course, is the familiar and specialized sense of pedagogy as a philosophy of teaching, including classroom practices and instructional methods, and the second is a more broad sense of pedagogy as education in general, of what the Greeks called *paideia*. On issues of suffering and how violence is connected to pedagogy, Worsham observes that critical theory in general has asked too few questions. For her, the increase in violence in the United States and elsewhere suggests that it is time to reconsider the real and symbolic function of violence. She argues further that while violence is commonly understood to occur at "the very limit of the social order where it displays the fragility of meaning, identity, and value," it "also (and increasingly) arises from within the authority of existing social, political, and economic arrangements and serves quite effectively to reinforce their legitimacy" ("Going" 215). A rhetoric of pedagogic violence analyzes the relationship between discipline and violence and focuses specifically on the ways in which "violence addresses and educates emotion and inculcates an affective relation to the world" (216). Because oppression and domination work not only on physical and psychological levels but on emotional and affective ones as well, ultimately "our most urgent political and pedagogical task remains the fundamental reeducation of emotion," and this cannot succeed by "mapping a new regime of meaning onto an old way of feeling" (216).

Scholars in feminist philosophy have been arguing for some time that *emotion* refers not simply to individual affective conditions but to, as Worsham succinctly puts it, "the tight braid of affect and judgment, socially and historically constructed and bodily lived, through which the symbolic takes hold of and binds the individual, in complex and contradictory ways, to the social order and its structure of meanings" ("Going" 216). Also, as Neil Nehring writes,

> Emotion, properly understood, is the whole works in evaluating a situation: our cognitive appraisals of it, our physical feelings about it, and our subsequent choices in expressing our approval or disapproval and acting on it. Knowledge is always accompanied by feeling, and vice-versa; we don't know anything about an event

> without feeling something about it and don't feel anything about
> an event without knowing something about it. (108)

Viewing emotion in these ways opens up possibilities for examining the social and political dimensions of those conditions and effects that have remained guarded by rhetorics of therapy within the psychological domain of the individual. How we feel about someone, something, or ourselves arises from social interaction and internalized assessment of both self and others. Affective responses are structural, political, and educable; they are able to be taught and learned in social contexts, and it is this pedagogic relationship to emotion that constitutes an affective relationship to the world or a kind of social-affective attunement. Viewing emotion in this way has particularly serious implications for the rhetorical study of cultural difference because it is often through emotions of assessment, both of self and other, that negative valuations of difference are affectively, effectively inscribed. In other words, how we feel about ourselves in relation to others is as much social and political as it is individual and psychological. Something we call gay pride, for example, is at once psychological *and* political: it is a move intended to counter collectively the effects of the internalization of stigmas of homosexuality as aberrant and pathological.

Working from the ideas of Bourdieu and Passeron, Worsham situates "dominant pedagogy" as the "power to impose meanings that maintain and reinforce the reigning social, economic, and political arrangements as legitimate" ("Going" 221). What is called "dominant pedagogy," then, is a "structure that produces individuals and groups who are recognized as such because they have internalized the legitimate point of view"; and, more than this, dominant pedagogy "depends on the social misrecognition of the objective truth of pedagogic work" (221). It is the primary work of dominant pedagogy, she continues,

> to organize an emotional world, to inculcate patterns of feelings
> that support the legitimacy of dominant interests, patterns that are
> especially appropriate to gender, race, and class locations. Peda-
> gogy locates individuals objectively in a hierarchy of power
> relations; but also, and more importantly, it organizes their affec-
> tive relations to that location, to their own condition of subordina-
> tion, and to others in that hierarchical structure. (223)

Further, the primary violence of dominant pedagogy is that its "primary pedagogic work mystifies emotion as a personal and private matter and conceals the fact that emotions are prevailing forms of social life, that personal life always takes shape in social and cultural terms" (223). Because emotion represents an assemblage of some of the more fundamental relationships to the self, the world, and others, the success of decolonization, more broadly thought of as projects of anti-sexism and anti-racism, depends, Worsham says, "on a recognition that the primary work of pedagogy is more fundamental than the imposition of a dominant framework of meaning"; decolonization and the struggle for social change, she continues, "must therefore take place at the primary level of emotion" (223).

Worsham further argues that critical theories and critical pedagogies have in large part failed to develop a particularly nuanced understanding of the affective dimensions of empowerment and disempowerment, as well as of attendant emotions such as humiliation, hatred, guilt, shame, anger, and pride. Much critical discourse does not apprehend its own limitation of the discourse of emotion, "what it places beyond the horizon of semantic availability," and, in this way, it does not make "emotion and affective life the crucial stakes in political struggle" ("Going" 235). She observes that with its rhetoric focused on pleasure and empowerment, "critical pedagogy works against itself to remystify not only the objective conditions of human suffering but also the varied experience of suffering" (235).

There is, however, a growing body of work on the complex interconnectedness of social and affective life, particularly on connections between emotion and power. Not surprisingly, feminist interest in anger and the politics of emotion has emerged over the last decade or so, represented in the work of scholars such as Ann Ferguson, Miranda Fricker, Morwenna Griffiths, Alison Jagger, Julia LeSage, and Elizabeth Spelman. Jaggar, for example, argues that women's anger is often viewed from the perspective of dominant pedagogy as a form of subordination subject to restraint because it suggests suppressed social relations and may become a source of political resistance and social change. Traditional understandings of the split between emotion and reason, wherein emotion is subordinated to reason, encourage dismissing women's anger as irrational or unfounded, something to be quelled, indulged, or patronized, but not taken seriously. Certain emotions—black anger, women's anger—must be put down, dismissed and/or individualized because of their transgressive potential, because they do not reproduce dominant pedagogical relations. In her important *Femininity and Domination*, Sandra Lee Bartky has traced the emotional and psychic dimensions of the phenomenology of oppression, at times working from the ideas of Fanon, to argue that the emotionally and psychologically oppressed become their own oppressors (22). As I will take up later in more depth, Audre Lorde and bell hooks have also studied how anger can be used productively and collectively to engage and upset the status quo. Lorde and hooks further argue that dominant pedagogy often works to keep black women separated from one another in ways that I will discuss later, thereby foreclosing collective healing as well as the kind of coalition building needed for social and political action. Such interrogations into the social, political, and pedagogical dimensions of emotion represented by Worsham, Bartky, Lorde, and hooks are important if we are to understand more accurately and deeply today's politics of difference and if we are to work toward a more affectively nuanced politics of engagement.

## Into the Heart of Whiteness

Making real, critical connections between affect and violence and among pedagogy, rhetoric, and emotions is all the more important in light of neo-conservative positions that seek to erase difference as a motivation for violence and, as a result, (re)mystify the pedagogic work of violence in policing dominant interests. A recent editorial of *The Economist* illustrates the line of thinking I am talking about. The writer argues, for example, that the general concept of hate-crimes is "incompatible with justice." Using the killing of James Byrd as an example, the writer argues that those convicted of hate-crimes should not get extended sentences. The writer says that

> The notion of "hate-crime" may be an extra penalty imposed on people whose views are offensive, as well as their actions. Ironically, it makes the justice system pick on them simply because they are different. . . . Even if bias exists in the system, the remedy cannot be to introduce racial weighting—or, indeed, weighting of any sort—into the concept of justice for all. (17)

It seems to me to be particularly difficult to support such a position in light of the realization that people have been killed and persecuted throughout history precisely because of their sexual, religious, and racial differences. Furthermore, "justice for all" has remained a myth to the victims of race-related and gender-related violence in all of its spectacular and mundane forms throughout the history of the United States. Such an argument ends up being little more that an apology for white supremacism and white violence, with all-too-familiar appeals to the First Amendment. The piece uses clearly racist and condescending language, arguing that those accused of perpetrating hate-crimes are being "picked on" because of their differences, their offensive views (in this case, white supremacist views), and arguing that blacks do not need "extra sympathy"—as if levying extended sentences against those convicted of hate-crimes is about giving "extra sympathy" to victims.

The crux of this troubling thinking is that there is a deliberate occlusion of difference in the analysis of the relations among violence, affect, and pedagogy. Put forth in place of such an analysis is an argument that rests on the belief that everybody should be treated equally, punished equally in this case, because to do otherwise compromises democratic ideals of fair and equitable treatment for all. The writer fails to take into consideration, however, that race- and gender-related violence and hatred are not exceptional, not pathological but deeply inscribed parts of dominant social relations. The fact of structural violence itself belies the fact that large groups of people are not being treated fairly based on their differences. But more than this, the omnipresence of structural violence suggests that violence is used to police dominant pedagogical relations— that violence is normal, normalized, and normalizing.

The writer of the editorial, in fact, dispenses with motivation of any sort for violence. In his view, violence just happens. Suppose Byrd were white, he continues, and had been the victim of three white youths looking to "indulge" in a little "aimless violence." Would that killing be less awful, the writer asks. Of course not, he answers. He continues, "yet hate-crime laws say that it would have been. The ghastly violence of the act is not seen as the nub of the problem (and the nub, indeed, of America's problem). Instead, race is" (17). The point missed here is that race and violence cannot be so neatly separated. (Were they ever able to be?) Contemporary definitions of race are ones that are intimately connected to imperial and colonial histories of displacement, colonialism, occupation, genocide, and slavery (although these genealogies of difference are often ignored and occluded in "multicultural" societies). And I need not rehearse the psychic and physical violence of slavery to make the point. According to the writer, violence is seen as a problem in itself, as if it is a thing that simply exists "out there," beyond people's minds, bodies, and feelings. As Worsham says, because dominant pedagogy posits violence and emotion as something beyond semantic availability and rational intelligibility, it mystifies its own pedagogic work as well as its use of violence to police dominant economic, social, and political interests.

Further, the writer argues that hatred can be "infectious": "If one man is seen to beat up a black, another may copy him" (17). Such a view posits an organic understanding of the operations of violence, in much the same way that other negative social phenomena such as racism and sexism are popularly understood: as strictly individual conditions that are perpetuated by a few reprehensible sociopaths. In this view, there is no structure or politics to affect, violence, and emotion. Violence is simply infectious, like a disease; it's a pathology that can be cured by letting it run its course. And what passes for pedagogical theory here is nothing more than "monkey-see, monkey-do," as if this were the way ideology as well as affective relations to the world and toward others are learned and taught. And how often has it been the case in the beating, mutilation, and lynching of blacks that a single white man is the perpetrator?

The only explanation offered is that violence just happens. Violence itself is the problem and not what motivates it. A particular kind of randomness of violence has been explained in popular media as well as postmodern theoretical discourse as *wilding*. Wilding, Worsham writes,

> entered the national vocabulary and the postmodern imaginary to describe the seemingly random acts of unmotivated savagery committed by bored and restless groups of youths looking for something to do. Wilding, by definition, seems to refuse to wear the face of poverty, race, gender, sex, or even madness. . . . Wilding is perhaps the predictable form violence takes when it is cut loose from affect: free-floating violence, so to speak, and its apparent randomness makes it seem purely anonymous and impersonal, even unintentional in the sense of having no proper object or aim. ("Going" 214, 231)

Viewing violence as "cut loose from affect" discourages analysis of the connections among violence and all sorts of axes of social identity. The definition of wilding mystifies "gender, race, class, and sexuality as the authorized tropes that name and mask the disfigured faces of hatred, bitterness, and rage" (231). Motivations for violence typically are put in psychological and individual terms or "cut loose" altogether from affect and defined as wild, random, and inchoate. Understanding violence as wild, random, or inchoate is perilous, however, because it discourages the study of the political and social dimensions of hate and violence.

The fact of the matter is that Byrd was not white and was dragged to pieces by white supremacists. He was not the victim of aimless violence, if there is such a thing. Violence may be misdirected, perhaps chaotic, but not aimless. Some may simply say that Byrd was at the wrong place at the wrong time, again erasing any motivation for the violence. As Carol J. Sheffield says of rape, however, such a wrong-place-at-the-wrong-time argument is inaccurate because it does not take into account the structural omnipresence of sexual and racial terrorism: "that one never knows when is the wrong time and where is the wrong place" (4). Byrd is a latter-day version of Foucault's "body of the condemned": he is a lesson, a person spectacularly tortured to death within a system that has used violence historically to police its social, political, and economic interests. Such a system continues to legitimate white violence and explain it away as aimless; requiring perpetrators to serve prison sentences, even extended ones, does nothing to upset this system. Byrd's death—as well as the harassment and death of others in the name of their differences—is a gruesome and tragic reminder of the pedagogic relationship between race and violence in the United States. Erasing difference as a motivation for violence is a strategy that works to conceal the fact that violence is used and has been used throughout history for political ends. Although the idea of hate-crimes does nothing to intervene in the pedagogic relations of violence, such an idea nonetheless is promising because it does signal a growing awareness that crimes are, in part and at some level, affectively motivated. The idea of hate-crimes also indicates that the psychological has run right up against the social and the political, necessitating the study of the social and political roles of violence in the affective relations of difference. That is, while I think the idea of identifying certain crimes as hate-crimes is not necessarily the answer to ending violence motivated by sexism, racism, and homophobia (how can it be since it does not disrupt or intervene in the workings of dominant pedagogy?), the idea of hate-crimes is a step toward linking conditions that are typically thought of as psychological and individual to social and political causes and effects. But dominant pedagogy hides the social, political, and pedagogic operations of violence and plays them off as something else, something psychological, something "wild," something extreme. What is needed is more than increased punishment for those convicted of hate-crimes; what is needed are new pedagogies, new affective relations to others, and new ways of feeling to accompany new ways of thinking. We need as well ways to differentiate effectively between a politics of hate and a politics of anger.

## The Different Politics of Hate and Anger

Because hate and anger are two of the more politically charged emotions, we would be well served to attempt to better understand how each operates in today's discussions of difference and engagement. To different degrees, hate and anger both can be thought of as emotions stemming from and protecting affective investments, those investments that incur strong feelings of protection—national pride, for example. Although there are overlaps in their affective registers, hatred and anger are not the same, and there are important differences between them that are worth exploring. Anger, for example, does not imply hatred, and anger may be used in both transgressive capacities (upsetting the status quo) and conservative ones (preserving the status quo). Because what we think of ourselves and others is *effectively affectively* inscribed into our hearts and emotions as well as our minds and thoughts, it is crucial to articulate more complex and politically oriented theories of the material and rhetorical effects of these intense emotions as they concern matters of cultural difference.

Post-Marxist theorist Chantal Mouffe makes a useful distinction between the terms "enemy" and "adversary": "'Antagonism' is a relation between enemies; they want to destroy each other. 'Agonism' is a relation among adversaries." She continues, "In the struggle among adversaries, you respect the right of others to have a different understanding of what citizenship is. . . . You respect the right of the opponent to defend his or her point of view" ("Rethinking" 180–81). Mouffe's distinction between enemy and adversary suggests helpful ways to distinguish between a politics of hate and a politics of anger. Whereas anger can be used to upset the status quo as well as maintain it, hatred can never truly be politically radical since it almost always involves scapegoating, isolationism, obsession, and cruelty. In part, the key to differentiating a politics of hate from a politics of anger may very well lie in distinguishing the social and political *abuses* of *antagonism* from the *uses* of *agonism*. We might see anger as a necessary part of the hegemonic struggle that makes up agonistic social and political relationships, part of the inevitable and unavoidable tension that forms relations among adversaries. Hate, however, would more accurately characterize relations of antagonism, relations between enemies bent on destroying one another.

Much psychological inquiry, however, does not explicitly connect individual or psychological conditions with social and political issues. The result is that psychology often identifies "problems" as individual and not social, and, consequently, the responsibility for curing these "problems" rests squarely on the shoulders of the individual. If the individual is "out of step," he or she must be brought "back in line" with the status quo in order to alleviate these problems. Therapeutic models seek to keep social relations as they are; change is good often only for the well-being of the individual. Dana L. Cloud writes,

> The *therapeutic* refers to a set of political and cultural discourses that have adopted psychotherapy's lexicon—the conservative language of healing, coping, adaptation, and restoration of a previously existing order—but in contexts of sociopolitical conflict. The rhetorical function of therapeutic discourses in such contexts is to encourage audiences to focus on themselves and the elaboration of their private lives rather than to address and attempt to reform systems of social power in which they are embedded. Thus, we can view the therapeutic as having restorative and conservative effects in the face of conflict and change. (xvi)

By individualizing the effects of alienation, exploitation, and oppression, psychology and therapy generally discourage public, collective forms of protest against the broader conditions of human alienation, exploitation, and oppression that are fundamentally social and political in nature. Although anger in much psychological discourse is not necessarily viewed as negative, it is, however, something to be relieved through catharsis, through the individual's channeling that energy toward creative or productive or at least non-destructive ends. In this sense, anger is typically not understood as an "essential political emotion" (Lyman 61) or as an impetus for thoughtful or positive social action, thereby discouraging interrogation of anger's relationship to the social and the political.

Effecting new ways of feeling, not just thinking, is one of the more fundamental ways of countering regimes of colonization and violence. Audre Lorde distinguishes between anger, "a passion of displeasure that may be excessive or misplaced but not necessarily harmful," and hatred, "an emotional attitude or habit of mind in which aversion is coupled with ill will" (152). Such aversion, it is worth repeating, does not come about naturally but is learned and taught, and in some cases explicitly trained. Speaking of self-loathing, a specific form of hatred, Lorde talks about how she was taught as a girl that a large segment of the population hated her because she was black and female. She describes overcoming the self-loathing that these lessons created in her as a long, deliberate, and difficult task:

America's measurement of me has lain like a barrier across the realization of my own powers. It was a barrier that I had to examine and dismantle, piece by painful piece, in order to use my energies fully and creatively. It is easier to deal with the external manifestations of racism and sexism than to deal with the results of those distortions internalized within our consciousness of ourselves and one another. (147)

As a process of identity formation, self-loathing is hatred turned inward and toward others similar to oneself. Instilling self-loathing in others is also a key strategy of racism and sexism and, thus, a powerful psychological form of social control, which, as Lorde observes, creates debilitating internalizations in the self.

Learning to hate oneself further ensures the development of barriers to establishing networks of mutual support and connection among members of the same disenfranchised group. Self-loathing serves the status quo because it discourages collective action, both in the capacity to heal and to resist. Bell hooks writes that black women are only able to make lifestyle choices that enhance well-being and reduce or eliminate debilitating stress if they believe they deserve to live well: "Most black women do not have this sense of 'entitlement.' We are not raised to believe that living well is our birthright. We have to claim it" (*Sisters* 60). Bartky observes that shame, an emotion of self-assessment, figures predominantly in the pedagogy of hatred; she is worth quoting here at length:

Under conditions of oppression, the oppressed must struggle not only against more visible disadvantages but against guilt and shame as well. It was not for nothing that the movement for black empowerment called not only for black civil rights and economic advancement, but for "black pride." Nor should we forget that this was the movement that needed to invent the slogan "Black is beautiful." What figures in much moral psychology as a disruption in an otherwise undisturbed life, is for whole categories of persons, a pervasive affective attunement, a mode of Being-in-the-world wherein their inferiority is disclosed to inferiorized subjects, though, paradoxically, what is *disclosed* fails, in the typical case, to be *understood*. Better people are not made this way, only people who are weaker, more timid, less confident, less demanding, and hence more easily dominated. The experience of shame may tend to lend legitimacy to the structure of authority that occasions it, for the majesty of judgement is affirmed in its very capacity to injure. The heightened self-consciousness that comes with emotions of self-assessment may become, in the shame of the oppressed, a stagnant self-obsession. Or shame may generate a rage whose expression is unconstructive, even self-destructive. In all these ways, shame is profoundly disempowering. The need for secrecy and concealment that figures so largely in the shame experience is disempowering as well, for it isolates the oppressed from one another and in this way works against the emergence of a sense of solidarity. (97)

Shame, guilt, and self-loathing can work to reinforce dominant pedagogy and the status quo in two ways: while discouraging collective identification and action, such emotions also help school people about themselves. Better people are not made this way, says Bartky, only ones more easily able to be dominated. In other words, people continue to allow themselves to be treated poorly because they have been made to believe that they deserve to be treated poorly; through the schooling of emotion, the oppressor teaches the oppressed to do the affective and psychic work of domination for them. Self-loathing turns the self and others like it into the enemy.

But the politics of hate also generate "external" enemies. Generating enemies is a process that functions in the development of group consciousness and group identity through identification and affiliation with those who hate similarly. Also, teaching people to hate and to see others as enemies is about dehumanization and the rationalization of violence. Psychologist Terrence Real talks about the similarity in the training of football players and soldiers, training that represents different instances of similar pedagogies of hate. In the case of the soldier, the pedagogical training involves national identification. The soldier is trained to dehumanize others, to objectify them, in order to be a professional killer in the state's employ, an employee who is expected to feel little or no remorse for actions carried out in the name of the state's political and economic interests. In football, he observes, players are taught that opposing players are "positions" to be taken out. This involves more than a stable team identification however, since players are expected to perform similarly for whatever team they play for; such pedagogical training also involves ideas and performances of masculinity. Real calls training in these cases the "conditioning out of empathy," which involves strategies of dehumanization and objectification that are also implied in war metaphors such as "necessary losses" and "collateral damage" (177). Training in the ways of "deadly competition" teaches and requires disconnection from the humanity of the opponent or enemy at the same time it teaches and requires disconnection from one's own affective and emotional structures or feelings.

A pedagogy of hate first empties affective and emotional connection both from the self and others and replaces these connections with a belief that others stand in the way of one's political and economic interests, of one's very life chances, and that the only way to deal with this untenable situation is to eliminate that threat. Violence often works in the service of hatred which can, as Slavoj Žižek observes, work in the service of the state or of a particular group either explicitly, as in the case of the training of soldiers, or implicitly by affectively policing dominant economic and political interests: "What bothers us about the Other is that he appears to entertain a privileged relationship to the object. The Other either possesses the object-treasure, having snatched it away from us (which is why we don't have it), or possesses a threat to our possession of the object" ("Leftist" 999).[1] A politics and pedagogy of hate creates enemies to be destroyed, taken out, subordinated. Hatred does not stem necessarily from anger, nor does it mysteriously and rancorously bubble up from the self. It comes from cycles of inferiorizing others, shaming them, and viewing them with contempt, from dehumanization and objectification.

Paying close mind to the politics of anger is all the more important once we begin to understand the conservative potential of anger as well as its transgressive potential, how anger "offers emotional resources to defend social order far more potent than ideology or reason" (Lyman 62). Anger in the conservative sense often results from widespread anxiety about changing social and economic conditions: "When the motive is the preservation of privilege we typically find the most violent anger, such as that directed by white heterosexual males toward gays, minorities, and women" (Nehring xix-xx). Nehring's thinking here aligns with Worsham's when she argues that while violence is commonly understood to occur at "the very limit of the social order where it displays the fragility of meaning, identity, and value," it "also (and increasingly) arises from within the authority of existing social, political, and economic arrangements and serves quite effectively to reinforce their legitimacy" ("Going" 215). One of the unfortunate results of the anxiety of changing times and roles is that white heterosexist male ideology has come to posit that "others" stand in the way of white heterosexual males' political and economic interests, of their very life chances, and that the only way to deal with this untenable situation is to eliminate or contain those threats. Anger is an integral affective component (in the enforcement) of dominant pedagogy and, for this reason, needs to be examined for its role in these conservative capacities as well as its transgressive ones. Also, Lyman examines anger as a socio-moral response that acts as

> the emotional foundation of civil order in its *moral* form, the capacity for moral outrage by which society defends its mores and sacred values. The moral response is trained, not learned; and it is intolerant, not flexible. It takes its power from the sense of personal violation that is aroused when one sees that which one cares for violated. The socialization of anger is an important part of the moral training of the good citizen. (62)

That is, the socialization of anger allows for the individual to serve authority and its interests uncritically, even perhaps to sacrifice one's own interests to that of authority (62). Viewing anger in these ways opens up critique of its role in social and political affiliations of all kinds, especially those stemming from patriotism and excessive national pride.

I hope that these distinctions between hate and anger, between enemy and adversary, point to ways that we can work toward a politics of difference that realizes the need for strong engagement as well as the transgressive uses of anger but that recognizes at the same time the crucial matter of countering pedagogies and politics of hate and their attendant regimes of terrorism and violence. Anger can be used in both conservative and transgressive capacities, and that is why it is so important to study it in relation to matters of cultural difference. On the one hand, the affective energy of anger over past and present atrocities can be used to interrogate the politics of differencing others and, on the other hand, it can be used to squelch differing and dissenting voices and to police the reproduction of "the same."[2]

## A Few Words about Hate Rhetoric

Referring back to the editorial of *The Economist*, let me say that the other argument being made is that any and all speech should be protected under the First Amendment: "It is not crime to hold such opinions [those of white supremacism] loathsome as they are" (17). The slippage between speech and action, however, comes in the next sentence: "The notion of 'hate-crime' may be an extra penalty imposed on people whose views are offensive, *as well as their actions*" (17; emphasis added). In this view, although it's illegal to engage in "offensive" actions (mutilation, murder), it's not illegal to hold "offensive" positions (all blacks essentially are inferior to whites) that may, in fact, lead to those very actions. The slippage here belies confusion about where rhetoric ends and action begins *legally*, as well as the fact that, as Catharine MacKinnon observes, "First Amendment speech and Fourteenth Amendment equality have never contended on constitutional ground" (73). The argument from both liberals and neo-conservatives alike that any and all speech should be protected under the First Amendment has become what MacKinnon calls "the speech you hate test":

> The more you disagree with content, the more important it be-
> comes to protect it. You can tell you are being principled by the
> degree to which you abhor what you allow. The worse the speech
> protected, the more principled the result. There is a faith that truth
> will prevail if left alone, often expressed in an openly competitive
> laissez-faire model taken from bourgeois economics and applied
> to the expressive marketplace: the "marketplace of ideas" meta-
> phor. The marketplace becomes the battlefield when we are
> assured that the truth will prevail while grappling in open encoun-
> ter with falsehood. (75–76)

What is feared in countering offensive speech, even hate speech, is the risk that such moves will become totalitarian, that they will be seen as censorship eroding the ideals of free speech. MacKinnon's objective is ultimately to get people to understand hate speech and expressions of racial and gender discrimination as violations of people's civil rights, thus exposing such speech and expressions to legal recourse. For our purposes in rhetorical and cultural studies, I think it is enough to see hate speech and expressions of racial and gender discrimination as politics and pedagogies of hate, as more than "offensive" (a term we might use in adversarial relationships) but as outright expressions of warfare (the language of a relationship between enemies). If rhetoric is symbolic action, as many in rhetorical studies think, if rhetoric has material and political effects in the world, then more attention needs to be paid to how rhetoric can act *materially* in negative ways. That is, hate rhetoric is more than just words; it has effects in the world, as it is intended to. Composition theorists, for example, have spent much time arguing that since rhetoric is symbolic social action, it can be put to use in order to argue for and create a less oppressive society. But in order to argue for and create a less oppressive society, we also need to articulate theories and pedagogies that are able to deal with the material effects of hate speech and not retreat from these issues because they happen to run up against ideals of free expression, ideals which often end up protecting more violent and extreme forms of expression rather than those marginal and dissenting voices already relatively powerless and inaudible.

## Writing on Eggshells

What is important to keep in mind is that we all manifest anxieties about uncertain social, economic, and political conditions in different ways, in ways that are informed by historical and social contexts, as well as by cultural codes, rhetorical conventions, social affiliations, and affective identifications. Furthermore, cultural differences often become the (re)production of signs of tensions and anxieties between groups. The difficulties faced in working against discrimination based on sexual orientation, ethnicity, gender, and race come from not only countering the systemic dimensions of these forms of discrimination. Difficulties also arise from attempting to communicate despite our differences in ways that do not foreclose collective action and in ways that realize that people's affective conditions and their anxieties, how they feel about others, have deep political implications.

Linda Alcoff discusses, for example, the price of coming to terms with white privilege: "'Feeling white,' when coupled with a repudiation of white privilege, can disable a positive self-image as well as a felt connection to community and history, and generally can disorient identity formation" ("What" 7). Such disorientation I see as both good and bad: good in that it can enable positive transformations of white identities; bad in that it can enable white backlash in the form typically of a politics of hate. While disarticulating and subsequently rearticulating white identities is necessary, it is important to realize that critiquing white ideology sets off deep affective resonances and uncertainties among whites about how to act. Feminist theorists such as Leslie G. Roman and Ann Russo, as well as Alcoff, have talked about the reactions of white feminists to black women's accusations of racism and to black anger. Alcoff discusses two primary reactions of whites in the face of such engagement: retreat and guilt. Of course, neither reaction is acceptable if we are to continue to counter oppressive regimes responsibly and reflexively. Both options leave the disenfranchised to work things out by themselves and are reactions afforded to some extent by privilege—whites can afford to do nothing; they can afford to leave things as they are. But retreat is not an option, as Alcoff suggests, because it significantly "undercuts the possibility for political effectivity" ("Problem" 107).

Guilt also can lead to disengagement from politics. When whites feel guilty about their involvement in racist structures, they often think that they have no role to play in the eradication of racism because they think they have nothing to contribute except more racism disguised by good intentions. Such a position, as Alcoff observes, in part rests on the assumption that "an individual can only know her own narrow individual experience and her 'own truth' and thus she can never make claims beyond this" ("Problem" 107). One of the problems with guilt is that it too undercuts the possibilities for political effectivity and for working across borders—forging alliances based on principles not only on biological and physical markers. Such reactions in the face of the difficulties of "speaking" with and to others is symptomatic of a condition wherein people often come to feel as if they are "writing on eggshells." That is, in my experiences I have observed that people (whites especially) are often afraid to say anything that might engage the deep affective charge underlying much of today's politics of difference, frightened to press positions too forcefully and shatter the thin shell of propriety. I agree with Alcoff that "we should strive to create wherever possible the conditions for dialogue and the practice of speaking with and to rather than for others" (110–11). Creating these conditions, however, involves in part realizing that our differences make for what Worsham calls "objective inadequacies": for example, since I am not black, I can never really know what that *feels* like ("Romancing" 570). But realizing objective or irreducible differences does not foreclose conditions for speaking with and to others; rather, such a realization presses us to seek critical and more creative ways to do this, ways that should be informed by histories and theories of difference and based on principles of critical negotiation.

Lorde talks about how whites in her experience want to be told what to do to fight racism. Not surprisingly, both Lorde and hooks have openly expressed impatience at such expectations that bespeak white privilege and often nothing more than good intentions. Lorde writes,

> Whenever the need for some pretense of communication arises, those who profit from our oppression call upon us to share our knowledge with them. In other words, it is the responsibility of the oppressed to teach the oppressors their mistakes. I am responsible for educating teachers who dismiss my children's culture in school. Black and Third World people are expected to educate

white people as to our humanity. Women are expected to educate men. Lesbians and gay men are expected to educate the heterosexual world. The oppressors maintain their position and evade responsibility for their own actions. There is a constant drain of energy that might be better used in redefining ourselves and devising realistic scenarios for altering the present and constructing the future. (115)

If white scholars, for example, are to engage in arguments to counter the effects of racism, then they cannot expect the privilege to be educated about how to do this (although they often do). In this sense, they cannot evade their responsibilities. Certainly, we must all listen, and listening is not the same thing as asking to be instructed. White people, for example, need to do their own theoretical and practical work to counter oppression, work that is messy and tough and involves heavy affective engagement. When engaging in such work, it should not be unexpected that one would meet the passionate and angry responses of others. Ultimately, theoretical and practical work, in this case, involves the kind of double consciousness for white ideology that I spoke of in Chapter Two; it involves identifying and countering white privilege while it seeks to create white identities that obscure neither positive nor negative aspects of white history.

Better understanding the relationships between rhetoric and strong emotions such as anger and hate is of enormous importance to the language work that we do in rhetorical and cultural studies, especially if we advocate dissensus- and conflict-oriented pedagogies as a way to confront inequities rather than avoid them. This is because how we argue for, write about, and conceptualize cultural differences are informed in large part by deep affective investments, by how we (are taught to) feel about one another. These feelings are not natural, nor are they purely psychological and individual. Thus, the politics and terms of any engagement cannot be fully understood without taking into account the intensely political and social dimensions of the affective relations of difference. Projects seeking to counter chauvinism, reductionism, supremacism, and elitism, in all of their spectacular and mundane forms, cannot succeed by merely mapping news ways of thinking onto old ways of feeling, to paraphrase Worsham. Neither can such projects fully succeed, I argue in the next chapter, if they do not rearticulate what we mean by "the therapeutic." That is, to counter the affective violence of difference there is a need to rethink shelter and safety in explicitly political and social terms and to connect the need for shelter in violent times to political and social issues of discrimination, engagement, and difference. How we think and feel about one another are political and pedagogical relationships, the terms of which must be relearned and rewritten if thinking and feeling that differences are reasons for the diminishment and exploitation of others are to be effectively resisted.

# Chapter Five

# From the Safe House to a Praxis of Shelter

> If we cannot identify the spaces in our lives where we are
> able to acknowledge our pain and express grief, we need
> to make them.
>
> —bell hooks

For the past several years, there has been much discussion in rhetorical theory and composition studies about the importance of "contact zones," conflict, and dissensus to the process of learning (Bizzell; Harris; Jarratt; Lu "Conflict"; Olson; Trimbur; West), but there has been less talk of the relationship between "safe houses" and conflict, as well as the roles strong emotion and anger play in social interaction and political engagement. Some scholars have argued that in order to help prepare students for participation in civic culture, it is necessary to articulate radical pedagogies, ones that encourage modes of argumentation and that see the tensions of cultural differences as points of political friction to be interrogated. In arguing for the necessity of agonistic pedagogical models, however, it is easy to overlook not only the affective relations of social and political engagement but also the fact that conflict and dissensus—precisely because of emotional ties and affective investments—do not always follow the proscriptions of reasoned or civil discourse, that engagement cannot always be understood in terms of prevailing rationalities and intelligibilities. In arguing for the importance of conflict to the process of learning (that ideological positions are forged and tested through argu-mentation rooted in cultural difference) it is also easy to ignore that sometimes we need to deal with some of the more damaging and long-lasting results of engagement: the effects of pain, violence, cruelty—psychic and emotional injury as well as physical damage. A. Suresh Canagarajah, for example, argues that proponents of recent critical pedagogies that focus on conflict and difference have tended to underestimate the necessity of working for "safe" forums for marginalized students of all kinds to exchange ideas and support one another (173). Furthermore, the social and political dimensions of anger remain largely undertheorized as they relate to issues of conflict and shelter. Issues of ideological conflict and shelter, in both social and pedagogical contexts, cannot be fully understood without examining the politics of anger, especially in its insurgent or transgressive sense. As I argued in the previous chapter, what is gained by paying close mind to the workings of anger and strong emotion in matters of cultural difference is a more affectively and rhetorically nuanced understanding of the politics of ideological conflict. And what is gained by paying close mind to the insurgent workings of anger in relation to shelter and "safe houses" is the possibility of articulating "a praxis of shelter," a critique and rearticulation of the therapeutic.

Much critical pedagogy typically has not focused on the necessity of creating and sustaining shelter in the face of deep and long-standing cultural hatreds. For this reason, it is important to advance ideas of shelter as they relate to dissensus pedagogies, at the same time that we attempt to better understand and counter such hatreds. In doing this, it might be helpful to conceive of shelter as something more than another kind of therapy, as a simple curing of the individual's problems so that he or she can be reintegrated into the status quo. In order to supplement traditional understandings of shelter as simply "safe places," I want to posit what I call *a praxis of shelter*. This is an admittedly difficult space that 1) seeks to foster social and political change from knowledge developed from within a community of suffering, and 2) attempts to rethink anger as a necessary component of such change. Shelter in this sense is not merely therapeutic, protective, and passive; it is political, transformative, and active. More traditional therapeutic notions of shelter are ones that seek to keep social relations as they are. Dana L. Cloud writes that the therapeutic, "as a situated, strategic discourse (or rhetoric), dislocates social and political conflicts onto individuals or families, privatizes both the experience of oppression and possible modes of resistance to it, and translates political questions into psychological issues to be resolved through personal, psychological change" (xix). By individualizing the effects of alienation, exploitation, and oppression, much rhetoric of therapy discourages public, collective forms of protest against the broader conditions of alienation, exploitation, and oppression that are social and political in nature. A praxis of shelter, however, seeks to politicize individual and psychological "problems" by attempting to understand the suffering and healing of individuals and groups explicitly in terms of social, political, and economic conditions. It also seeks to understand anger in social and political terms, rather than in just psychological ones, and works to channel the affective energy of anger over conditions of alienation, exploitation, and oppression toward the development of alternative perspectives and thoughtful social action.

## Complicating the Safe House

Some scholars have evoked Mary Louise Pratt's idea of "contact zones," hoping to theorize a pedagogy that takes the tensions of multicultural societies as productive of dialogue, deliberation, negotiation, and reflection. But little attention has been given to what Pratt refers to at the end of the same article as "safe houses." She writes, "Where there are legacies of subordination, groups need places for healing and mutual recognition, safe houses in which to construct shared understandings, knowledges, claims on the world that they can then bring into the contact zone" (40). Undoubtedly, creating and sustaining places to heal from legacies of oppression is crucial, and Pratt's call for such spaces is welcome and needed. Joseph Harris, however, has productively complicated and extended Pratt's idea of the safe house, pointing to a need to theorize the connections between contact zones and safe houses more explicitly:

> [Pratt] is left in the end with no real answer to the question of how one constructs a public space in which the members of various "safe houses" or affinity groups are brought into negotiation (not just conflict or contact) with other competing views and factions. Or, to put the question in terms of classroom practice, Pratt never makes it clear how a teacher might help students move between the exhilaration and danger of contact zones and the nurturance of safe houses. (119)

For Harris, Pratt talks too little of any kind of relationship between sites of contact and those of safety; in other words, what is missing from her descriptions both of the contact zone and of the safe house is any kind of talk of their co-constitutive interdependence.

What Harris has in mind is a more thorough articulation of the theoretical and practical relationship between the two sites than Pratt provides. Describing his work with African-American students, Canagarajah makes clear the pedagogical implications of the safe house and articulates well the interdependent relationship between sites of contact and those of shelter:

> While safe houses offer a measure of protection from the tense inter-cultural engagement of the contact zone, they are not cut off from it altogether. The safe house is not a passive site that simply provides psychological relief for marginalized groups; it is a radically active site that generates strategies and resources to transform the dominant discourses in the contact zone. It is not a politically-free or neutral site that helps marginalized groups take leave of struggles over power and difference; it is a subversive site that nurtures oppositional perspectives, demystifies dominant ideologies, and breeds constant friction with established discourses for their democratization. The safe house is integral to the contact zone—not only for its success as a site of multivocal text production and emergent discourses, but for its self-definition as a meeting point of heterogeneous cultures and ideologies. The two sites are then interactive and interdependent, while being antagonistic. Though each site influences life in the other, the influence of the dominant structures in the contact zone is hegemonic while that in the safe house is potentially resistant. Hence the pedagogical significance of safe houses. (195)

Canagarajah's work is important because he points to crucial ways that we can begin to extend Pratt's thinking on safe houses, ways in which to nuance our understanding of safe houses and shelter in relation to dissensus pedagogy and cultural difference. I would add, however, that it is crucial when discussing issues of cultural difference, conflict, and shelter that we also take into account the role of anger in conflict because of the inextricable emotional and rhetorical relationship between anger and conflict. Anger should not be ignored in discussions of the relationship between conflict and shelter precisely because anger can act as an impetus for thoughtful social action; in fact, anger is often the first step toward developing alternative perspectives necessary for action and change.

As Pratt sees it, the safe house is a place where the friction caused by zones of contact is suspended by mutual consent for the sake of respite. As I see it, however, because of deep affective charges, that kind of friction cannot be easily and temporarily put on hold, so to speak, but is more productively interrogated and examined within the safe house. So, to view the safe house as not a zone of contact itself is to avoid the friction that makes the safe house necessary in the first place. My praxis of shelter, however, seeks to put that friction squarely into the realm of analysis.

Developing pedagogies that take into account the connections between anger and conflict challenges us to rethink anger in explicitly political and social terms, not only in the individualistic terms of much psychological and therapeutic rhetoric. As I will address more fully later, it might serve us well to confront the "challenges" of anger by, among other things, developing strategies that emphasize perseverance in the face of confrontation and patience with those of alternative views. In these ways, we might encourage ideological conflict and productive argumentation without implicitly condoning hostility, invective, and personal attack.

### Anger and/in the Classroom

Near the end of "Arts of the Contact Zone," Pratt asks, "What is the place of unsolicited oppositional discourse, parody, resistance, critique in the imagined classroom community?" (39). But given the agonistic dimensions of contact zones and dissensus pedagogy, I think it is also important to ask, What is the place of unsolicited anger, hostility, rage, and invective when dealing with issues of cultural difference? And, how do we as instructors engage such strong emotions? Susan Jarratt has suggested that by avoiding thorny issues and conflict as a pedagogical operation instructors may be "insufficiently prepared to negotiate the oppressive discourses of racism, sexism, and classism surfacing in the composition classroom" (106). I would add that separating the study of conflict from the study of anger is perilous because such analyses artificially divorce conflict from its tense emotional and rhetorical content. By deemphasizing anger in analyses of conflict, instructors may be insufficiently prepared to deal with the high emotions that often accompany talk of racism, sexism, and classism in the classroom. In a recent article, Andrea Greenbaum offers an interesting study of anger in the classroom. Her study, I think, highlights the need to rethink the emotional "problems" and outbursts of individual students in more explicitly social and political terms for the purpose of imagining pedagogies based on theories of the interconnections of conflict, shelter, and anger.

Greenbaum relates that while engaging in peer review in class, a white student, Brian, reviewing the paper of a black student, Johnnie, pointed out that he was using idiomatic spelling of dialogue inconsistently. Taking this as an accusation that he couldn't spell, Johnnie became angry and accused Brian of racism, saying that the accusation that he can't spell rested on the fact that he is black. Despite Brian's attempt to reassure Johnnie that it was merely a matter of inconsistency, Johnnie did not back down, and the other black students in class ended up rallying around him. Greenbaum writes,

> Instantly, the class had divided along racial lines, with the African-American students *erupting in shouts* to Brian that he was racist and that his comment was inappropriate. Not surprisingly, the white students sided with Brian, *arguing* that his question was a legitimate one and that his job as editor and facilitator was to bring up all matters related to the text. (2; emphasis added)

Overwhelmed by the reality of engaging collective black anger as a white woman instructor, and sensing that she had lost control of class, Greenbaum dismissed the students.

Johnnie never returned to class, and Greenbaum says that she never discussed the situation further with the rest of the students. Working from postcolonial theory about issues of representation and who speaks for whom, Greenbaum spends much of the rest of the article reflecting on the connections between literacy and cultural identity. She suggests that within the political act of peer critique "the intensity of the racial rift had to do with the perception by my African-American students that Brian's comment was an attempt to colonize their personal language—an effort, whether intentional or not, to diminish and denigrate their cultural, political, and social reality" (4). She goes on to identify Johnnie's paper, "A Life in Harlem," as a "subaltern text," and argues that Brian's "accusation" suggested that Johnnie didn't have basic literary skills. Interestingly enough, Greenbaum ends by saying that Johnnie did indeed have a kind of agency: he disrupted the "colonist desire to create literacy in its own narcissistic image" at the same moment that that desire was reinforced. She concludes: "In that volatile instant, Johnnie wrenched me away from the mirror, forcing me to divert my gaze from the lure of my own reflection" (8).

Certainly, Greenbaum is correct in identifying the force of black anger, but she does not see this as collective and political, only something to be feared and avoided. It is Johnnie she believes who wrenched her away from the mirror of her own narcissistic image of literacy, not the collective political force of black anger in the classroom. Many whites are not accustomed to black anger, especially collective black anger and, consequently, are unable to understand it in any kind of political sense; a common response is to dismiss it as dangerously irrational. I am not so concerned here with who is right or who is wrong but with the social, economic, and political pressures ensuring the insularity of "minority" politics, interests, and anger. Whites are not accustomed to dealing with such anger and politics precisely because structural arrangements make it so they do not have to. Certainly, the description of the white students "arguing" their positions and the black students "erupting in shouts" is symptomatic of political relations and structural arrangements in the country in general.

I am not questioning the validity of Greenbaum's description, but what I am saying is that such descriptions are at once stereotypical and accurate. They are stereotypical in the sense that they jibe with racist representations of "out of control minorities." But such descriptions are accurate for what they tell about the frustration and impatience felt by those whose economic and political interests are not being represented and how that frustration and impatience is read as irrational and incoherent. That is, those of disenfranchised groups often feel angry and display strong emotion, not because they are essentially emotional and hence unreasonable, as racist arguments go, but because in part their participation in politics is, at best, systematically discouraged. Left unanalyzed, such displays of strong emotion reinforce racist beliefs of "out of control minorities." The "reasoned" arguments of the white students, on the other hand, indicate to some degree their general ease and familiarity—though not necessarily facility—with dominant political conventions of negotiation and debate, as well as faith in such a system that relies on these conventions. Left unanalyzed, the cool, acceptable arguments of the white students stand in stark contrast to the characterization of "minorities" who cannot control themselves. Also, the white students' defensive position reflects the increasingly defensive postures—in this case polite, but in others extreme and hostile—of whites in and outside of the academy. In addition, I think many whites are surprised to realize that black anger could be directed at them, a situation that makes them ask: What did *I* do? Such a response, again, is the result of viewing race relations and racism in purely individualistic terms: *I* didn't do anything; why be angry with *me?* The point is that anger in the classroom represents macro- as well as micropolitical articulations of anxieties about social and economic conditions. Anger, in this case, should not be seen as something merely psychological and individual (Greenbaum ascribes the force of anger to Johnnie alone) but as something collective and political. The issue is not so much to determine whether Johnnie was right or wrong or to attempt to justify or condemn his actions but to attempt to understand better the affective politics and investments that figure into engagements of difference, politics and investments that do not always follow "reasoned" and civil proscriptions.

Greenbaum's classroom clearly was no safe haven for anyone: for the black students feeling intellectually threatened, for the white students feeling verbally assaulted, or for the instructor feeling inadequate in the face of such a highly emotionally charged politics of difference. Proposing a negotiation of perspectives in such a case, however, is troubling. A move toward negotiated consensus represents an attempt at the kind of easy reconciliation and integration of perspectives that I think avoids tough questions and the political content of expressions of anger. What is to be done then? I think it is important in these cases to use imagination critically and creatively so as to think outside of "reason" and approach issues and impasses in ways that may be occluded by more accepted, mainstream, or "reasonable" approaches. It is important also to recognize here the tight braid of emotion, conflict, and cultural differences and to begin to think about ways to learn from such situations and to put that learning into practice. Taking the tensions of social difference as starting points for interrogation of social and political issues is imperative. To do this, however, it is important to attempt to meet the challenges that anger presents. Meeting these challenges must include rigorous theoretical and historical analyses of social and political issues in order to supplement the "authority" of students' personal experiences concerning matters of cultural difference. It is also necessary to foster patience and perseverance and the ability to listen to others. Using these strategies does not undercut the politics of anger and ideological conflict that I am talking about but, more precisely, discourages knee-jerk emotional reactions and encourages understanding anger politically and rhetorically. I think by better understanding the insurgent role of anger in conflict, anger might be used more effectively and accepted as a part of conflict that doesn't necessarily include outright hostility or personal attack.

## Engaging (the Political Dimensions of) Anger

But what are the forms our responses could take in response to collective and political anger? I think that strategies of patience, perseverance, and the ability to listen to others can be used without undercutting ideological conflict or deflecting anger. These strategies are not meant as ends in themselves or as easy answers, but as ways to begin to clear the air for honest talk on social issues, talk that should be historically and theoretically informed. In this matter, Catherine Clinton's "Contents Under Pressure: White Woman/Black History" is illustrative. In it, Clinton describes the difficulties and complexities of working as a white woman in black history. She describes responding to the many interrogations by blacks and whites about what a white woman is doing in black studies. Her response is that while she realizes that she is "objectively inadequate," as Lynn Worsham would say ("Romancing" 570)—that she is not black and can never know entirely what that *feels* like—nevertheless her ongoing work in and commitment to the field give her a kind of right to be there. Furthermore, it is not only experiences and biology that constitute one's position but theoretical work and commitment as well. As Linda Alcoff observes, believing that one can speak only from and for one's own group, in part, rests on the assumption that "an individual can only know her own narrow individual experience and her 'own truth' and thus she can never make claims beyond this" ("Problem" 107).[1]

But as Clinton illustrates, doing and being committed to such "crossover" work involves more than doing one's homework; it involves becoming thick-skinned and acting from the realization that emotional and affective investments are just as important as professional ones—that emotional and affective investments, in fact, often motivate professional and personal agendas more than reasoned choices do. She describes cultivating patience, perseverance, and a sense of humor in the face of hostility, as well as the capacity to listen to others. For example, she writes,

> Despite the very hard and at times tragic circumstances surrounding black men and women confronting extraordinary obstacles to having an ordinary semester, a sense of humor seems my most strategic asset for teaching and learning. Blacks are more willing to listen if I laugh at myself ("melanin-impaired"), and whites are better prepared to face their shortcomings if they are stung by wit rather than full frontal assault. (248)

Also, she describes how her relationship to black women colleagues and professionals continues to be complex:

> Many black women academics who don't know me stereotype me and build up a wall between us as they lay eyes on me. At conferences there have been threatening questions from the audience, covering a range from "You're a honky bitch and I'm not" to "Who do you think you are?" I have learned, especially with people I don't know who enjoy lecturing me on the basis of my skin color rather than on what I have to say, the value of letting other people have their say, just let it all spill out. If their ideas seem to me to be particularly racist or mean-spirited, I might attempt a reasoned response. *But too often it's not what I've said, it's what they haven't been allowed to say.* Offering them the unimpeded opportunity to challenge my views can clear the air and perhaps lead to dialogue and future communication. (252; emphasis added)[2]

Too often the responses to anger are dismissal or avoidance—*disengagements*, in effect, from the political. But anger is not always something to be avoided or dismissed or answered with more anger; it is not always a bad thing. As Audre Lorde says, "anger is a passion of displeasure that may be excessive or misplaced but not necessarily harmful" (152). And anger is not hatred, nor does it always bespeak hatred, as is commonly thought. Certainly, the anger felt by Clinton's black colleagues is understandable; it stems from a feeling of being invaded: you're encroaching on our territory. But there is more going on here than a mere policing of disciplinary boundaries. The issues that Clinton describes are informed by the complex and tense historical relationships between white and black women in the United States, of who speaks for whom, from the power differentials of slavery to the exclusion of black women in the earlier stages of feminism. The anger of black women toward white women in this case stems, in part, from exclusion not only from expression but also from channels of social and political action, from critique, deliberation, and self-definition. This is why white responses to black anger— demonization, avoidance, retaliation, dismissal, guilt—are wholly inadequate and counterproductive to passionate and thoughtful dialogue. None of these reactions seek to understand the affective and emotional implications of being systematically denied political voice.

In situations in which anger erupts in the classroom, perhaps listening to and letting anger be expressed is one of the better responses. Of course,

Johnnie's anger was not directed at the instructor but at another student. But I wonder if such anger can be redirected to initiate discussion and writing about cultural differences. After all, feeling angry is often the first step toward action and change. I remember a Cuban woman in one of my classes talking about experiencing racism. She and her mother had been referred to in racist terms, perfectly audibly, by a white woman as they were all waiting in a cashier's line at a department store. The student was visibly upset as she related the encounter, and after she was finished we all sat in silence, no one knowing exactly what to say. A white student suddenly blurted out, "That was probably my grandmother!" At this, the entire class erupted in laughter, even the student relating the experience. Someone had said something that defused the anger in a way that did not dismiss or ignore it, in a way that cleared the air for some honest talk about racism and about how we can communicate on difficult subjects despite our differences. The white student wasn't joking and subsequently began to reflect on growing up surrounded by racist ideas. In this case, I may have been fortunate that someone had used humor in a way that kept discussion moving in a tense and honest manner, but clearly we cannot rely on such defusing remarks.

But how else can we begin to understand the complex affective investments and political articulations of anger if we don't listen? If we dismiss anger as unreasonable? If we avoid and ignore it? If we don't make our classrooms "safe" for tense discussions, ideological conflict, alternative perspectives, and engaged writing? As Clinton suggests, I think we can employ strategies of perseverance, patience, listening, and humor (not in the sense of nervous deflection, but in the sense of being able to laugh at ourselves, not taking ourselves too seriously) in conjunction with rigorous historical and theoretical analyses in ways that do not undercut the ideological productivity of conflict and argumentation, ways that, nonetheless, might help to diminish untempered hostility and outright invective.

It may be true, as Greenbaum writes, that at the moment when Brian exposed Johnnie's inconsistent spelling "the historical reality of African-American oppression—in all its sundry forms—merged" (6). But it might also be accurate to say that in having what he felt as his inadequacies exposed in front of his classmates, Johnnie felt embarrassed. Sandra Lee Bartky, Worsham, and others talk about shaming as a powerful psychological form of social control. Perhaps Johnnie felt he was being shamed, and, certainly, as Greenbaum observes, this involves issues of literacy and race. Once having drawn a line with anger, backing down would have seemed like further shaming, like an affront to investments in both his masculinity and his blackness in his and his classmates' eyes. This is not to uncritically justify such investments; rather, it is to argue for putting the connections between such investments and anger squarely in the realm of analysis. It also would be helpful when listening to others, to attempt to *think* emotion and not merely *feel* and react to it, to try to understand how anger can act as a dialectic of self and world. Because anger can be used in both conservative *and* transgressive capacities, it is a deeply political emotion. And for this reason, it is important to better understand how anger works both in pedagogical and social forums as they relate to matters of cultural difference and shelter.

## Toward a Praxis of Shelter

Like Canagarajah and Harris, I do not see the idea of shelter as separate from a pedagogy of the contact zone but as an interdependent part of it, as a site necessary for the political articulation of emotion and passion for social and political change. If pedagogical theories based on conflict, dissensus, and engagement are to be advanced, then I argue that they need to be advanced in dialogue with discourses on healing, shelter, and trauma. Such theories might elaborate on "therapeutic" responses to engagement—on treating the immediate effects of conflict, for example—but also on the idea of shelter that questions dominant therapies' understanding of the split between the individual and the social, the psychological and the political. In "Writing Trauma, History, Story: The Class(room) as Borderland," Daphnae Read writes that the "radical imperatives of teaching in the borderland include facing trauma" and that "trauma challenges the traditional separation between the academic realm of the intellectual and the private realm of experience" (112–13).

I suggest focusing on collectively dealing with the trauma and the wounds of the violence of oppression without reinforcing the idea of the therapeutic as strictly healing, the intention of which is often the reintegration of the individual into the status quo. Also, we might rethink use of the term "safe house" in these contexts. For starters, one of the more unsafe places can be, in fact, the household. One of the more fundamental types of shelter is shelter from violence that occurs within the home—that of physical, emotional, psychic, and sexual domestic violence. "Safe" can work also in two ways: in the sense of being *safe for* and being *safe to*. That is, although a shelter may be safe *for* victims of oppression because it offers them protection, it may also be safe *to* structures of oppression because it does nothing to question or upset those structures. If a shelter is safe *to* systems of oppression and violence, then the work of that shelter, although necessary and laudable for its sheltering work, does not challenge the systems of oppression and violence which are its *raison d'être*. Such a "safe" shelter remains caught in, and in some ways supports, cycles or economies of violence and healing.

Adrienne Rich also identifies two distinct connotations of the word "safe": safety can imply "a place to gather our forces, a place to move from, not a destination"; but there is also "the safety of the 'armored and concluded mind,'" the safety that "becomes a dead end in the mind and in the mapping of a life or a collective vision" (206). Also, one of the pitfalls of pedagogical models of nurturance, Worsham observes, is that such pedagogies of nurturance "work alongside (often cheerfully) radical pedagogies of critique and confrontation to reproduce and reauthorize the affective relations typical of the middle-class nuclear family and thus constitute the latest version of the family-education couple" ("Going" 237). Such pedagogies of nurturance are manifestations of regimes of therapy that perpetuate an economy of violence and healing precisely because they do not intervene in patterns and cycles of violence. Further, such nurturance mimics western medical models because it emphasizes treating and healing the effects of violence rather than working to end its causes—that is, like western medical models, these pedagogies of nurturance target the acute but not the chronic.

The phrase "safe house" also suggests that shelter has been modeled after the private work of the household and is thus the duty of, specifically and traditionally, women. The potential danger here is that such language can serve to reemphasize that it is women who should perform the physical and emotional labor of tending wounds in primarily non-professional and "nursing" capacities. The language of the "safe house" can help to reinforce rather than upset both the sexist and individualistic nature of therapeutic regimes of western cultures, regimes that discourage the collective action primarily of women. A praxis of shelter, instead, suggests theoretically-informed pedagogies broadly conceived that do not simply reinforce traditional notions of healing and nurturance or posit shelter as an escape or a home. A praxis of shelter further works to expose "the therapeutic," the restorative and conservative dimensions of regimes of therapy, because the therapeutic offers "help" primarily to the individual and often works against collective action by seeking to restore the individual to his or her place in the order of things. Above all, such a praxis posits sites of shelter and healing as places to regroup for further engagement, spaces where the anger of past and present atrocities may be rearticulated into thoughtful, collective social action that resists enabling the conditions requiring such shelter in the first place. I am thinking about praxis in generally a Marxist sense: of theoretically-grounded activity aimed toward the transformation of an unjust world. And I am thinking of shelter as being limited, temporary, active, and provisional. After the initiation of shelter, it either becomes a component in the dominant cycle of violence and healing, because it does nothing more than heal, or it becomes something else, a new social collective or political bloc from which the affective energy of anger and suffering may be mobilized for social change.[3]

The idea of a praxis of shelter rests on two primary premises: 1) that people are motivated to act socially and politically because of their affective conditions and investments, and 2) that suffering is one of the fundamental motivations for human community and action. Chantal Mouffe argues that people are not so much motivated to act collectively by their reasoned interests as much as they are by passion: "We need to understand the dynamics of those passions in order to realize that it's very important not to try to erase those passions or, as some would say, relegate them to the field of the private" ("Rethinking" 196). Similarly, Homi Bhabha thinks that "the discourse of political action and political choice has concentrated too much on questions of interest and too little on questions of political passion" ("Staging" 34). The passion then shared by those of a shelter designed for protection, by those dedicated to resisting the forms of oppression that put them there is, according to Mouffe and Bhabha, deep and enduring social and political motivation.

We must realize that nothing but the endless wounding and scarification of consciousness can be accomplished through relentless engagement and antagonism. Therefore, we must work somewhere between Fanon's imperative to fight violence with violence and therapy's refusal to intervene in economies of violence and healing; this somewhere is a praxis of shelter, not an "in-between" space meant as an easy reconciliation or as a mere integration of perspectives or positions, but a theoretically informed practice that recognizes the need for protection and healing while it encourages public, collective forms of protest against the broader conditions of human alienation, exploitation, and oppression.

## The Challenge of Anger

In discussing the relevance of ideological conflict to learning and in attempting to reimagine pedagogical and social forums that allow for the wrangle of differing positions and perspectives, it is crucial to take into account the role of anger, if for no other reason than because anger is the fundamental rhetorical and emotional component of conflict. The thoughtful articulation of anger, however, is also crucial for a praxis of shelter to succeed, for shelter to become active and transformative. Furthermore, if shelter is to be thought of as an active rather than a passive site, as Canagarajah suggests, then it would seem that a move from an *arts* of the contact zone to a *praxis* of shelter is necessary. That is, rather than only studying texts of contact zones, it might be helpful if we supplemented this approach by paying critical attention to the micropolitics of the classroom as Harris suggests. He says that the difference between an "arts" of the contact zone and pedagogies of difference rooted in classroom practice is that

> rather than representing life in the contact zone through a set of ideal texts or suggestive yet brief classroom anecdotes, such work populates it with the differing and sometimes disturbing writing of actual students. The contact zone thus becomes . . . a description of what we now often actually confront in our classrooms: a wrangle of competing interests and views. And the goal of pedagogies of the contact zone, of conflict, becomes not the forcing of a certain "multicultural" agenda through an assigned set of readings or lectures but the creating of a forum where students themselves can articulate (and thus perhaps also become more responsive to) differences among themselves. (123)

Becoming more responsive to differences requires, as Clinton illustrates, intense focus on the rhetorical and political intricacies of anger. Rethinking anger in rhetorical and political terms becomes especially crucial because conflict does not exist without its emotional complement of anger. Indeed, acting as if the two are separable can lead to sanitizing and romanticizing conflict; sanitizing conflict would mean ridding it of its "messy" emotional component, and romanticizing it would mean not taking into account conflict's harmful and damaging fallout.

Imagining anger as a productive political intervention in pedagogical and social forums is admittedly difficult. And thinking of ways to implement shelter to make use of anger for the purpose of fostering oppositional and alternative perspectives is as equally difficult. And I admit that what I am talking about is more theoretical than practical. But I'm not simply saying that it's acceptable for students to get angry in the classroom, only that if we advocate and practice conflict-oriented and dissensus pedagogies, expressions of anger in the classroom should not come as a total surprise, nor should such expressions be considered in purely individual and psychological terms. Also, it is important when studying the politics of engagement and difference that we consider rhetoric not only as the marshalling of *logos* but as the strategic display and restraint of emotions, especially anger, for social and political ends.

Pratt has initiated a way of thinking about shelter that has been productively extended by both Harris and Canagarajah. As Canagarajah puts it, "while safe houses offer a measure of protection from the tense inter-cultural engagement of the contact zone, they are not cut off from it altogether. The safe house is not a passive site that simply provides psychological relief for marginalized groups; it is a radically active site that generates strategies and resources to transform the dominant discourses in the contact zone" (195). I hope too that rethinking the safe house in terms of a praxis of shelter will help us to better envision forums able to accept and engage the challenges of anger, forums that do not tolerate, however, politics of hate, a politics characterized by scapegoating, isolationism, obsession, and cruelty. *A praxis of shelter* thematizes the relationship among conflict, shelter, and anger, and it encourages productive tensions between differing ideological positions while it recognizes the necessity of shelter as an active site of both protection and resistance.

# (Against) Conclusion

## Taking It Outside, or, Rhetoric and Politics Beyond the Pale

> The struggle for ideological and political hegemony is always the struggle for the appropriation of the terms that are "spontaneously" experienced as "apolitical," as transcending political boundaries.
>
> —Slavoj Žižek

In part, this book has been about critiquing liberal and rationalist rhetorical-political procedures 1) for the ways in which they screen out the disruptive aspects of emotion, passion, and irreducible differences, and 2) for the ways in which they sell democratic ideals as the norm and attempt to frame partisan debates in nonpartisan ways. In Chapter 1, I critiqued traditional notions of negotiation as compromise, the art of the deal, and forwarded a "double-edged" process of *critical negotiation*, a model of engagement that sees negotiation less as a mere dealing and more as a postcolonial dialogic process. In Chapters 2 and 3, I argued for a critical negotiation of perspectives concerning issues of race and gender. The rhetorical politics of cultural difference, I further argued in Chapters 4 and 5, work on deep affective levels, so it is important to pay close mind to the politics of emotion and the emotion of politics. In this chapter I would like to sketch directions for further study and discussion of the rhetorical politics of "othering," or labeling positions and arguments as "outside" because they do not fall in line with the normative rhetorical and political criteria of civility and liberal-democratic procedures and politics. In arguing for the right to be different—creatively, critically, and variously—it is crucial to advance rhetorical politics of difference that accept differences on their own terms and that critique liberal-democratic procedures themselves as sources of conflict, even though, ostensibly, their objectives are often to reduce conflict.

In rhetoric and politics, to be "outside" often is to be considered loud, brash, dangerous, unintelligible, unreasonable—even evil; in short, it is to be considered extreme, anything that helps define a position as non-rhetorical or non-political, as unworthy of a sincere hearing and ineffective by established standards. To "take it outside" is to remove forms of disruptive action, to dismiss general mixing it up, from the "inside"— those spaces and forums of convention, propriety, etiquette, and manners. Civility, similarly to the politics of negotiated consensus, must be considered critically as a form of rhetorical othering because civility is not just about manners and etiquette but can also be about squelching difference by delineating normative criteria for inclusion and interaction. In fact, calls for negotiation that I critiqued earlier in this book can be seen in the larger context of calls for civility in general. Critics of incivility in governmental relations and public life argue that renewed commitment to the principles and conventions of civility can help to revitalize public discourse on justice. Proponents of civility, such as Robert Putnam and David Broder, recommend a return to civility in our public discourse and think that incivility is eroding a sense of common justice, precisely because justice is seen as largely based on the communicating conventions of civil society: on politeness, propriety, and etiquette. However, the crucial problem with the notion of justice based on civility and propriety, as Mark Kingwell says, is that "armed with a theory of justice turning on propriety, we can always indulge the luxury of labeling threatening political behavior 'uppity'" (231–32). Kingwell suggests that we adhere not necessarily to "common," democratized "polite" conventions but that we commit to understanding deeply and politically one another's positions. As he observes, just because someone is polite or civil does not necessarily indicate that they have any interest in understanding someone else's point of view.

What is needed is further inquiry into how the rhetorical politics of "othering" manage difference and reduce the possibilities of the disenfranchised taking on subject position forcefully. Justice should not be based on strict normative criteria but on the inclusion of differences that may stress normative criteria and alter the social and political landscape. I want to make it clear that I'm not saying simply that civility is always and everywhere "a tool of the oppressor," but that the conventions of civility, like those of negotiation, have much to do with classist and "interested" notions of propriety. In this sense, those with the power to institute their ways with language can use civility, among other things, to restrict forceful arguments and/or alternative perspectives by outlining normative criteria for interaction and politics. Of course, there will always be criteria for community and inclusion by definition, but social justice should be based not on propriety and civility but on accepting differences on their own terms and on continually questioning the normative criteria that serve to limit the critical potential of difference. I think that radical and contingent politics as articulated by theorists such as Ernesto Laclau, Chantal Mouffe, and Judith Butler, as well as by recent postcolonial cultural politics, can suggest directions for a hermeneutic of political rhetoric that teases out the contradictions of democratic ideals and procedures vis-à-vis practice.

## "The Politics of X" and Political Contingency

Theorists such as Judith Butler, Nancy Fraser, Ernesto Laclau, Chantal Mouffe, Joan Scott, Iris Marion Young, and Slavoj Žižek—to name only a few—have been preoccupied with articulating workable and varied conceptions of politics in times of increasing delegitimation of progressive and leftist critical projects. Many also express concern about the general depoliticization of public life. Part of the problem in attempting to repoliticize things may lie with the fact that "politics" is overused, a floating signifier in critical discourse devoid of any truly descriptive power and open to anyone's private, dehistoricized spin on its definition and role. Diana Fuss writes that politics "represents the aporia in much of our current political theorizing" and that, "paradoxically, politics often occupies an *apolitical* position in our thinking—a position of unquestioned power and privilege" (105). Fuss goes on to rehearse a certain weariness from the avalanche of papers, books, and conferences entitled "The Politics of X." However, the "growing discontent with the failure to historicize politics itself should not lead us on a quest to locate the 'true' identity of politics" (105). Fuss worries that "deference to the primacy and omniscience of Politics may uphold the ideology of pluralism, for no matter how reactionary or dangerous a notion may be, it can always be salvaged and kept in circulation by an appeal to political strategy" (106–07). Fuss makes it clear that she is not suggesting that we do away entirely with arguments of tactical or strategic necessity, but that the easy recourse to political stratagem currently needs to be rethought: "Perhaps the question we must always keep before us is: 'politically strategic *for whom?*'" (107).

For postmodern thinkers, Fuss' proposition of questing for a "true" identity of politics is loaded, but it does not mean that we should not, in fact, attempt to historicize politics and risk definitions of the political, ones that seek to re-politicize rather than de-politicize things. The point is not for such definitions of the political to be held up as the only "true" ones, but to articulate them so that they can be contested and played against others, critiqued and argued for so that, in effect, they can become political and politicized. Žižek contends that there is a politics proper, not a "true identity" of politics but a sense that politics is about relationships (or more accurately, non-relationships) to the social edifice: "political conflict proper involves the tension between the structured social body, where each part has its place, and the part of no-part, which unsettles this order on account of the empty principle of universality" ("Leftist" 988). For this idea of politics he goes to ancient Greece "when the members of the demos (those with no firmly determined place in the hierarchical social edifice) presented themselves as the representatives, the stand-ins, for the whole of society, for the true universality" (988). He continues, "The political struggle proper is therefore never simply a rational debate between multiple interests but, simultaneously, the struggle for one's voice to be heard and recognized as that of a legitimate partner" (989). What Žižek is trying to do is imagine a leftist appropriation of the Western legacy of politics in order to repoliticize things, to wrest control of what politics has come to mean away from what he calls the "cultural logic of multinational capitalism," of models of politics based on technocratic schemes of negotiation ("Multiculturalism").

For Žižek, the risk associated with the negotiated, interest-group, political logic of multiculturalism, for example, is that it papers over the real conflicts of difference and, as a result, helps stage a return of the repressed political, not in the form of agonism among adversaries, as Mouffe would have it, but in the form of a politics of hate:

> At the very moment when, according to the official ideology, we are finally leaving behind the "immature" political passions (the regime of the "political"—class struggle and other "out-dated"

divisive antagonisms) for the "mature" post-ideological pragmatic universe of rational administration and negotiated consensus, for the universe, free of utopian impulses, in which the
dispassionate administration of social affairs goes hand in hand
with aestheticized hedonism (the pluralism of "ways of life")—at
this very moment, the foreclosed political is celebrating a trium-
phant comeback in its most archaic form: of pure, undistilled racist
hatred of the Other which renders the rational tolerant attitude
utterly impotent. In this precise sense, contemporary "postmodern"
racism is the *symptom* of multiculturalist late capitalism, bringing
to light the inherent contradiction of the liberal-democratic ideological project. Liberal "tolerance" condones the folklorist Other
deprived of its substance—like the multitude of "ethnic cuisines"
in a contemporary megalopolis; however, any "real" Other is
instantly denounced for its "fundamentalism," since the kernel of
Otherness resides in the regulation of its *jouissance*: the "real
Other" is by definition "patriarchal," "violent," never the Other of
ethereal wisdom and charming customs. One is tempted to
reactualize here the old Marcusean notion of "repressive tolerance," reconceiving it as the tolerance of the Other in its aseptic,
benign form, which forecloses the dimension of the Real of the
Other's *jouissance*. (37)

The political impulses repressed by the interest group model of multicultural
politics return as regressive fundamentalisms, as intense gender and race
hatreds. Because these extreme positions fall outside political logic based
on ideals of negotiated consensus and civility, they are dismissed as
irrational, as incomprehensible, as evil—as specifically *not* political.
Repoliticizing models of politics based on negotiated consensus would
allow us to see so called reactionary and fundamental positions in a
political sense and not dismiss them outright as evil and incomprehensible. Certainly, reactionary and fundamental positions may advocate
abhorrent or distasteful viewpoints and methods, but dismissing these
positions as non-political, as outside of politics is itself a disengagement
from politics that more often than not serves to sanction strong-arm or
violent countermeasures.

Iris Marion Young discusses other ways that the politics of interest-
group pluralism serve to depoliticize public life. She claims that such a
depoliticized "political" schema equalizes claims for justice:

In the process of conflict resolution, interest-group pluralism
makes no distinction between the assertion of selfish interests and

normative claims to justice or right. Public policy dispute is only
a competition among claims, and "winning" depends on getting
others on your side, making trades and alliances with others, and
making effective strategic calculations about how and to whom to
make your claims. One does not win by persuading a public that
one's claim is just. This strategic conception of policy discussion
fosters political cynicism: those who make claims of right or
justice are only saying what they want in clever rhetoric. This
cynical system often forces movements claiming justice, like the
civil rights movement or the movement for the Equal Rights
Amendment, to identify themselves as merely another interest
group. Those who believe in the justice of equal rights for women
must form pressure groups to get what they want, and be prepared
to deal and bargain to get it. (72)

The political schema that Young refers to erases and flattens difference
and, in turn, posits all groups and movements—social, business, political,
ethical—as merely interest groups. Such a strategy not only effectively
ignores how differences have been historically constituted and continue
to operate in the political landscape, but it further assumes that all
"interests" carry equal moral and ethical weight. This is not to posit some
hierarchy of ranked claims wherein one is deemed more or less important
than others; rather, it is to realize that the idea that all claims are equal is
an ideal that erases difference and depoliticizes claims to justice. Through
a similar move, uncritical multiculturalism posits cultures as equal by
ignoring genealogies of difference or the historical production of alterity
that continue to have drag in the present. Claims to justice, simply put, do
not carry the same ethical and moral weight; they have different histories
and different connections to politics, to business, and to civil issues; they
have different actors and different stakes. But laboring under the ideal that
smokers' rights, let's say, are as equally morally valid as civil rights strips
a concept of social justice of any critical edge by dehistoricizing and
depoliticizing all claims to rights, by reducing them to those of equal
competing interest groups.

The idea of "radical democracy" articulated by Ernesto Laclau and
Chantal Mouffe in *Hegemony and Socialist Strategy*, and since elaborated
upon, holds promise for revitalizing and re-politicizing democratic ideals.
Radical democracy involves highlighting and exploiting the tension of
the logic of democracy: between the logic of popular sovereignty and the
universalist logic of pluralism (Mouffe, "Rethinking" 186-87). Democracy, in short, relies on the logic of exclusion: "For democratic citizens to

be able to express their sovereignty, you need to have a *demos* and the *demos* needs to have people who are not part of the *demos*" (187). But all this needs to be articulated within a universal discourse of human rights, which moves toward the logic of universal inclusion. Of course, an idea of universal inclusion would undermine the possibility of democracy. The point here is that democratic ideals are wonderful, but they do not exist in practice. What is required is a return to a sense of "the political," and to a politics that recognizes that a completely harmonious society is impossible. This means that agonism, conflict, and exclusion are inevitable and unavoidable, and that pluralism can never be totally inclusive; it can only be limited. The aim of radical democratic politics, according to Mouffe, is to create institutions in which conflict does not take the form of an antagonism between enemies who want to destroy one another but instead takes the form of hegemonic agonism among adversaries who respect one another's competing notions of citizenship.[1]

For Judith Butler, Laclau, Mouffe, and Žižek, radical and progressive politics must deal with the idea of "the universal" and "the particular" at the same time: "Politics always involves a kind of short circuit between the universal and the particular; it involves the paradox of a singular that appears as a stand-in for the universal, destabilizing the 'natural' functional order of relations on the social body" (Žižek, "Leftist" 988–89). Butler thinks that procedural or substantive notions of the universal, ones that do not see the category of the "universal" as a site of insistent contest and resignification, are perilous and so has forwarded a notion of politics based on the idea of "contingent foundations":

> We have witnessed the conceptual and material violence of this practice in the United States's war with Iraq, in which the Arab "other" is understood to be radically "outside" the universal structures of reason and democracy and, hence, calls to be brought forcibly within. Significantly, the U.S. had to abrogate the democratic principles of political sovereignty and free speech, among others, to effect this forcible return of Iraq to the "democratic" fold, and this violent move reveals, among other things, that such notions of universality are installed through the abrogation of the very universal principles to be implemented. . . . To herald that notion [a procedural or substantive notion of the universal] then as the philosophical instrument that will negotiate between conflicts of power is precisely to safeguard and reproduce a position of hegemonic power by installing it in the metapolitical site of ultimate normativity. . . . A social theory committed to democratic

contestation within a postcolonial horizon needs to find a way to bring into question the foundations it is compelled to lay down. It is this movement of interrogating that ruse of authority that seeks to close itself off from the contest that is, in my view, at the heart of any radical political project. (7-8)

What is clearly needed is a sense of the political as contingent, a politics that does not rely on uncomplicated notions of the universal nor on ones that seek to universalize—ironically, through force if necessary—the ideals of rational, negotiated consensus.

The assertion of the universality of agonism and reflective knowledge in no way suggests, as Žižek puts it, that "in social life, there is no dialogue, only war" ("Multiculturalism" 51). It means, instead, as Mouffe suggests, that the political must allow for and insist on the "agonistic struggle among different understandings of citizenship" ("Rethinking" 179) while cultural-rhetorical politics that seek to turn political adversaries into hated enemies be critiqued at every turn. Such a political space, then, should be one thought of as allowing for and insisting on something between negotiated consensus and outright warfare—on a radically contingent sense of hegemonic political agonism.

### The Politics of Cultural Composition:
### Toward a Multi-Critical Rhetoric of Difference

Civility is about, at some level, restricting political registers, and, for this reason, what is needed as well as a study of rhetorical othering is a re-politicizing of political rhetoric in multicultural and global contexts. Because "culture" is connected to notions of "civilization" and "civility," it is crucial to consider civility's connection to *culture*. Raymond Williams observes that the complexity of *culture* is a source of great difficulty for any modern theory of culture and that "the problem of knowing, at the outset, whether this would be a theory of 'the arts and intellectual life' in relation to 'society,' or a theory of the social processes which create specific and different 'ways of life,' is only the most obvious problem" (17–18). Two of the most important problems are culture's association with "civilization" and language, and what is important for guiding my questions here is the connection of culture to "civilization" and to the constitutive role of language; I am concerned with the roles of civil discourse and thought in defining and delineating the terms and limits of "acceptable" difference. Modern ideas of civilization, and by association civility, have been constructed over and against ideas of "uncivil others" in colonial contexts: "At the same time as the question of cultural difference emerged in the colonial text, discourses of civility were defining the doubling moment of the emergence of Western modernity. Thus the political and theoretical genealogy of modernity lies not only in the origins of the *idea* of civility, but in this history of the colonial moment" (Bhabha, *Location* 32). The idea of culture-as-civilization historically has equated civility with politically and morally "mature" cultures and incivility with "savagery" or politically and morally "immature" or "backward" cultures, thereby relegating them to the nonpolitical, to a culture justifiably dealt with by means outside "civil" politics—by violence, oppression, or occupation, for instance. Today's corollaries to such "uncivil civil" politics operate in the form of such U.S. injunctions, especially toward Middle Eastern nations and cultures, to shape up and negotiate—or be bombed.

Working toward what we might call a *multi-critical rhetoric of difference* involves, among other things, approaching culture—like race and gender—as a specific kind of "ideology of difference." It involves exploring how *culture* continues to function as the difficult medium through which people construct images of themselves and others, images that in turn affect social and political policy. I think it is important to supplement current understandings of multiculturalism with a sense of a "transcultural heterogeniety," wherein the prefix "trans" connotes co-constitutive relationships among cultures, along with a hermeneutic of cultural rhetoric that focuses on how cultures are created *in difference, as difference.* Such a hermeneutic allows for a way to think of *culture* as infused with difference, dissent, and agonism in order to recognize the transformative potential of, as Bhabha puts it, "culture's in-between"— the hybrid, third space of cultural translation, wherein "culture" is co-constituted or mutually inscribed or critically negotiated in relations of difference. Bhabha thinks that engaging the political dimensions of the idea of culture itself necessarily involves politicizing processes of cultural differentiation in post- and neocolonial contexts so as to argue against, as he says, the naturalization of the notion of culture:

> Cultural difference is a particular constructed discourse at a time when something is being challenged about power or authority. . . . Cultural difference is not difficult, if you like, because there are many diverse cultures; it is because there is some

particular issue about the redistribution of goods between cultures, or the funding of cultures, or the emergence of minorities or immigrants in a situation of resources—where resource allocation has to go—or the construction of schools and the decision about whether the school should be bilingual or trilingual or whatever. It is at that point that the problem of cultural difference is produced. So, it's really an argument against the naturalization of the notion of culture. ("Staging" 16)

For Bhabha, a cultural politics that looks closely at processes of cultural differentiation is about critiquing arguments for rights and interests based on appeals to coherent cultural traditions (the politics of multiculturalism). This is because coherent cultural traditions are based on the naturalization of the notion of culture, on the idea that culture is organic and self-generated rather than political and multi-determined. Such a cultural politics further seeks to expose the operations within genealogies of difference and politics of alterity that give rise to coherent cultural traditions from which claims for rights and interests are made.

The problem with multiculturalist notions of society as consisting of diverse and balkanized cultures is that all groups appear to have their own, self-generated cultures, and, coupled with democratic ideals, all cultures are seen to have equal opportunities and equal articulation in American political culture. Cultures are not typically seen as being constituted relationally *in difference, as difference*. As Nancy Fraser puts it,

> Pluralist multiculturalism tends to substantialize identities, treating them as given positivities instead of as constructed relations. It tends, consequently, to balkanize culture, setting groups apart from one another, ignoring the ways they cut across one another, and inhibiting cross-group interaction and identification. Losing sight of the fact that differences intersect, it regresses to a simple additive model of difference. (185)

What Fraser refers to as additive models of difference are those ways of conceiving of cultures as relatively self-contained and self-generated social items that can simply be "added" to one another, like beads on a string, to form a "multicultural" society. The fictional and partial dimensions—nonetheless formidable—of these cultures as well as how they are defined through interaction with other cultures are typically not interrogated. It is this lack of questioning the very "composition" of culture(s) and the processes of cultural differentiation that has led to the apolitical "politics" of multiculturalism or "parapolitics" of which Žižek speaks. Such a parapolitics largely sees groups and cultures as discrete social units with equal opportunities in the political landscape; consequently, these "politics," according to Žižek, disavow political agonism in multicultural contexts in favor of schemes of interest-group negotiation. In light of such a treatment of culture, a "cultural politics" needs to be cast that advocates and fosters a hermeneutic of cultural rhetoric that engages the co-constituted dimension of *culture* from various critical and "minority" positions.

Thinking of culture as difference necessarily involves, Bhabha argues, focusing on postcolonial and migratory conditions and contexts in particular as a way to disrupt the genealogical purity of cultural and national histories. Because of the transnational dimensions of social transformation—displacement, relocation, occupation, migration, diaspora—it is crucial to take into account postcolonial critical perspectives which require, as Bhabha says, "forms of dialectical thinking that do not disavow or sublate the otherness (alterity) that constitutes the symbolic domain of psychic and social identifications" (*Location* 173). Similarly, Fredric Jameson talks of *culture* as the relationships involving the material and affective "transactions" among groups and the necessity, therefore, when studying culture to realize the "constitutive role of the boundary" or the way each group is defined by and defines the other (33).

Furthermore, by not being critical of processes of cultural differentiation we ignore the historical constitution of difference, genealogies of difference that are suppressed both by a non-differential concept of cultural time and by present-day ideals of equality. Bhabha thinks that the recurrent problem with liberalism's notion of equality is that liberalism works from a non-differential conception of cultural time:

> At the point at which liberal discourse attempts to normalize cultural difference, to turn the presumption of equal cultural respect into the recognition of *equal cultural worth*, it does not recognize the disjunctive, "borderline," temporalities of partial, minority cultures. The sharing of equality is genuinely intended, but only so long as we start from a historically congruent space; the recognition of difference is genuinely felt, but on terms that do not represent the historical genealogies, often postcolonial, that constitute the partial cultures of the minority. ("Culture's" 56)

Normalizing cultural difference through historical amnesia, a starting over from a clean slate, is another aspect of the rise of a multicultural, interest-group, political schema wherein groups argue for rights and interests based on group affiliation that comes to be naturalized through appeals to a coherent culture. That is, culture comes to be (seen as) the basis for fairly coherent and organic group identity for the purpose of arguing for rights and interests within a political scheme largely governed by the rules and conventions of negotiated consensus. What is at issue today, Bhabha writes, "is not the essentialized or idealized Arnoldian notion of 'culture' as an architectonic assemblage of the Hebraic and the Hellenic" ("Culture's" 53). What is crucial, he thinks, is that culture is understood as something co-constructed by groups in situations of post- and neocolonial engagement. No group, Fredric Jameson also says, "'has' a culture all by itself" (33). Culture is, among other things, about anxieties of difference in relation to others:

> For culture—the weaker, more secular version of that thing called religion—is not a "substance" or a phenomenon in its own right, it is an objective mirage that arises out of the relationship between at least two groups. This is to say that no group "had" a culture all by itself: culture is the nimbus perceived by one group when it comes into contact with and observes another one. It is the objectification of everything alien and strange about the contact group. . . . "Culture" is the ensemble of stigmata one group bears in the eyes of the other group (and vice versa). . . . Still, it happens that "we" also often speak of "our own" culture, religion, beliefs, or whatever. These may be identified as the recuperation of the Other's view of us; of that mirage whereby the Other has formed a picture of us as "having" a culture. . . . Culture must thus always be seen as a vehicle or a medium whereby the relationship between groups is transacted. ( 33–34)

Such "mirages" or "alienated images" demand responses, and depending on the power of the Other, these responses may take a variety of forms. The point here is that culture is more productively thought of as a relationship among groups wherein investments of various sorts—political, economic, affective—influence the circulation of social and linguistic meaning in highly charged arenas of semiotic and political representation. To put it simply, people don't go around saying "I am of this or that culture" unless they have a reason to define themselves as part of a group in relation to other groups for political and economic purposes.

*Culture*, as we have come to think of it, does not inhere within someone or something, but neither is it entirely and coherently group-generated; culture is generated between and among groups, within language, along asymmetrical lines of access to the means of political representation and cultural production. Bhabha is especially concerned with these kinds of cultural transactions in relation to "minority" cultures: "In contemplating late-liberal culture's engagements with the migratory, partial cultures of minorities, we need to shift our sense of the terrain on which we can best understand the disputes. Here our theoretical under-standing—in its most general sense—of "culture-as-difference" will enable us to grasp the articulation of culture's borderline, unhomely space and time" ("Culture's" 55). Thinking of "culture-as-difference" involves a study of *cultural composition*, the rhetorical study of the anxieties of groups concerning the increasing globalization and "mongrelization" of seemingly originary cultures:

> Fewer and fewer cultures are originary; fewer and fewer cultures can identify any stable lines of continuity between their origins and the present. The more we know about all these cultures, including the ones that do their best to preserve their internal homogeneity, the more we understand how diverse their sources are, how much they've been influenced by others, how much they've borrowed across the borderlines. The borders have all been porous. So, our condition, the condition of all of us—even people who haven't moved an inch—is to discover our increasingly diverse cultural composition. (Hall, "Cultural" 176)

Rhetorics of cultural composition in this sense seek to understand how "cultures" and identities are "composed" *in relation to* other "cultures" and identities. Such a line of thinking requires us to see culture as an assemblage of relationships, formed within the asymmetrical politics of difference. The critical project according to Hall becomes examining the production and effects of "myths of homogeneity, of purity" vis-à-vis the reality of a "mixed, mongrelized world" (177). Hall writes that the diasporic experience, for example, is a "figure for the increased pluraliza-tion of cultural forms and for the insistence that culture works not by perfectly reproducing itself into infinity, but precisely by *translating between*" (177).

Examining the myths of the coherence of culture in relation to global-wide social transformation is crucial to understanding culture as the multiple interpretations of difference among groups, as well as the co-constitutive role of language in the composition of culture. Further, such a cultural rhetoric would 1) see culture as a site of anxiety and source of conflict, 2) assess the role of emotion and political passion in the formation of culture(s), politics, and identities, and 3) examine the interlocking effects of environment, nationality, sexuality, gender, class, and race on the formation of consciousness and on social and political policy. Such a cultural rhetoric would bring together analytical and critical functions whose aims are transformative, different versions of rhetorical and critical traditions the aim of which would be to imagine alternatives—alternatives perhaps dauntingly difficult to imagine from originary theoretical positions—to extant coercive regimes.[2]

Postcolonial figurations such as Hall's "diasporic experience" and Bhabha's "colonial migration" are important for infusing studies of cultural composition with a sense of critical difference from "minority" perspectives. What *cultural composition* in this sense becomes is a kind of post- and neocolonial rhetorical studies that examine the uses of discourses of authenticity to create and affirm "cultures" from which to articulate particular politics for particular reasons. The kind of *multi-critical rhetoric of difference* I have in mind involves taking a stance that advocates *re*composing and sustaining social relations based on the ability to listen to and for others, on learning to speak with others, on fostering a multi-critical fluency, on encouraging strong mutual critique, on developing critical negotiation, and on working against the historical legacies of imperial and elitist enculturation as well as the continually shifting logics and alliances that constitute, often globally, present-day forms of cultural imperialism.

*A multi-critical rhetoric of difference* recognizes that there is an increasing need to be critical of struggle concepts, or signs of struggle, such as *culture*, as well as the contradictions of liberal-democratic concepts and procedures. It is pressing to reconsider cultures as "compositions of difference" by fostering states of knowledge that are prepared to suffer modification and interrogation by what they neither posses nor can claim as their own (Chambers 50). All this requires critical and radical rhetorics, critical and radical literacies, contingent politics and forms of cultural-rhetorical politics concerned with issues of contested definitions of citizenship articulated in post- and neocolonial contexts, and that practically and theoretically engage both fundamental regressivisms and the omnipresent interest-group political logic of multiculturalism.

# Afterword

# Risking Action at the Edge of Understanding

## Peter Vandenberg

*Where do we go from here?* When Thomas West asked me to write the Afterword to *Signs of Struggle*, he offered me this question as a heuristic. It put me in mind of an anecdote I have told before, an extended figure, really, for groping around at the edge of understanding: While I was working on my B.A., I shared a small, two-bedroom bungalow with Victor, a black, domestic long-haired cat. Victor liked to run, continuously. He'd start racing at the front of the house under the picture window, tear through the small living room and dining room, down the short hallway, across the kitchen, and up onto the window ledge at the rear of the house. And then back he'd go again. Over and over. He was lithe, agile, confident. But a desire to break out exceeded his mastery of the familiar. When the back door opened he was always there, desperate to escape through the crack between my leg and the door. Full-speed through the back yard he would go and then, just a few feet from the edge of the yard, stop. Dead in his tracks, he would just stand there facing out across the alley as if up against some transparent boundary. I would follow him out, pick him up, and carry him back inside.

Eventually, I just let Victor go when the door opened. I could throw away the trash or move the sprinkler, and he would just stand there at the end of his run, somehow *trans/fixed*. Eventually I would walk over, pick him up, and carry him back inside. I don't know how long this went on

121

before I realized that the distance he covered on his way to the alley was almost exactly the same distance he could run in-doors. I suppose that like Victor, we all tend to patrol our own areas with confidence and assurance, yet we have a driving desire to break free from the space marked out in our heads by some routine authority of restriction. And, like Victor, wherever we go, there we are again, having dragged the customary template with us into the unfamiliar. It is out here along the perimeter of our own understanding where we engage in signs of struggle. This is where differences are constructed, where one complex of rituals, habituations, and ways of knowing generates heat in contact with an/other. We know this, of course, and we're familiar with the sort of paralysis Victor's story represents—to move is to inevitably extend one's entire geography of meaning; to move is to encroach, implicate, and other simultaneously. To his credit, Tom West offers us no easy way out of Victor's dilemma. By refusing the rubrics of *diversity* and *multiculturalism*, West shows us that efforts to engage difference have too often collapsed into compositions of the familiar, grounded in the ironic topoi of authority—pluralism, rationalism, consensus, tolerance, civility.

Instead, West reminds us that the deep structure of dominant-culture assimilation, for those authorized by it, is both powerfully resilient and nearly imperceptible. The cherished liberal principles that we wish were only applied with greater equity turn out, on examination, to be the difference-erasing mechanisms that sustain hierarchy and injustice. In a culture of "diversity," West argues, acceptable markers of difference are revealed as those that constitute the least significant threat to engines of hegemonic control. *Critical* differences, those that would disrupt business as usual, are effectively neutralized by protocol for public interaction so thoroughly fundamental to a "civil society" that it is understood to be self-evident. For those of us occupying positions of privilege in dominant-culture institutions, then, working for any sort of meaningful change may first require a critical exploration of the habitual and familiar, the terrain where footing is so sure. This, of course, is where oppression, discrimination, and essentialist thinking are structured into patterns of the everyday.

Steering a course between so-called "natural equality" and nativistic retreat, West embraces threat, contestation, disruption, and dissensus on the way toward "expanding the ground rules for risky interaction" (5). Centered on unveiling ways in which our most routine interactions suppress critical differences, he theorizes critical negotiation and hybridity as deliberate strategies of resistance and translation; later he proposes a rethinking of "shelter" in terms of a "political, transformative, and active" praxis designed to restructure "individual and psychological 'problems'" in relation to "social, political, and economic conditions" (123–24). This is strong, important, potentially transformative theory. But good theory, as we now conceive it, is limited—by its inability to travel well outside a privileged discourse, by limiting structures of dissemination, by the inevitability of generalization and its distance from local, material conditions. Good theory today, like many usefully corrosive compounds, requires an activating agent.

So, where do we go from here? To work. As individuals—as intersections of competing discourses of domination and resistance—we need to find sites in which to *enact* transformative praxis, to *trans-figure* the theory of critical negotiation into the act of negotiating critically, to use the range of discretion we control to carry out a "praxis of shelter." We need to embrace the element of risk that West elaborates, and those of us who risk less in material terms by engaging in transformative praxis face an obligation to do more on behalf of those who risk more. But this call to action must first be a call to interrogation lest we bypass West's crucial call for a "reconceptualization of the *civitas*" (19). We need to recognize and address the leveling functions of institutional practices, and the terms through which difference-erasing procedures are unselfconsciously constructed and carried out as a matter of routine.

Hip-deep in the often dissimulating rhetoric of Diversity and Multiculturalism, those of us working in higher education have much to do. The job search, for example, is typically a space in which a professed desire for difference is washed away by the institutionalized requisites of *expertise* and *collegiality*—both of which, as markers for business-as-usual, can function to suppress the sort of conflict that may lead to change. If mass education in the West reflects the residue of the imperial project on a massive scale, the job search is a key moment in an individual academic's long march of compliance. In the sometimes crass play of liberal identity politics under the rubric of Diversity, departments are often rewarded for interviewing "one of these" (African American, Latino, Pacific Islander) as they search for "one of these" (medievalist, dramatist, compositionist). Such an approach is grounded in what West calls "racial thinking," and tends to further entrench a pluralist or conservative agenda. When the first category is not understood or encouraged to have a reconstitutive effect on the second, the procedure annuls the threat of critical difference; on a level the hiring department often does not acknowledge or perceive, candidates must effectively demonstrate that the particular class of difference they bring will not significantly challenge, or color, the department's sense of what constitutes expertise in a given field.

We might also turn a critical eye to the transition from job *candidate* (one who seems likely to come to a certain fate) to *colleague* in a painfully lengthy term of *probation* (a period of proving fitness as member of a group). To all but the most fervent initiates, the long march to academic tenure can seem like the mother of all normalizing procedures, a machine for the eradication of alternative potential. Tenured faculty might explore the possibilities, where and when we can in our own departments, of reimagining mentorship as something less like lubricating new faculty for the mechanisms of assimilation and more like what West calls a "praxis of shelter." As I understand it, West proposes a conception of shelter as an actualized attitude—an active effort to flip over procedures and occasions of standardization so that they become metaphorical spaces in which to practice critical difference. Those of us who enjoy the limited protection of tenure could do much to make department meetings and committee assignments "active site[s] of both protection and shelter" (West 142). Too often new faculty, particularly women and those of color, function in such situations as little more than fodder for consensus on the positions of those with greater authority. Their role in such circumstances is often limited to displaying evidence of collegiality. Senior faculty actively engaged in a praxis of shelter might create conditions that would allow critical differences to flourish and make change.

In looking to enact a praxis of shelter, we must follow West's lead and recognize the classroom as a space immediately open to our influence, a fertile field of "application." Yet we must continue to explore the disjuncture between the homogenizing impetus of education—particularly literacy training—and our desire to stimulate change. As teachers who inevitably assign, grade, and take attendance, we are unavoidably positioned to reinforce civil-society conditions that undergird a patriarchal, racist structure. The task of exposing the normalizing, difference-erasing effects of this framework is so difficult because the critique is played out within it, leaving the teacher who does not confront this problem head on in a position of nearly inescapable bad faith. We must, it seems to me, make this immediate, pressing, and complex tension *the* ongoing focus of critical negotiation in the classroom.

We can have an impact on other classrooms, too, particularly those of graduate students and adjunct faculty, by finding ways to make the discourse of theory more open and accessible to them. As publishing academics critical of systems of domination that stratify and divide, we need to find ways to do theoretical work while critically negotiating criteria for academic success grounded in publication, which effectively *other* faculty engaged primarily in teaching. We must take great care to extend the conception of scholarly activity beyond the metaphor of mere *conversation* and, as West has done here, toward a conception of scholarship as a mechanism that can compel social and political change. Teachers, those with an aptitude for engaging and desire to engage others in "practical" situations, will embrace work they perceive to be oriented toward action. How they do this, of course, will depend on the circumstances in which they work. We need to walk a careful line, avoiding grand claims for the efficacy of theory and too-easy pronouncements about its limitations. If published theory has value for those of us who want to make critical change, then we must begin to reconceptualize it as something more like an instrument rather than an institution.

This will demand that we attend to the implication of theoretical work in patterns of domination and control. We need to collate the desire to compose an "agonistic or tense plurality" (7) rooted in conflict, struggle, and the threat of disruption with the critique of *agon* recently undertaken by feminists in rhetorical theory. We must also continue to strive for a widening of perspective in the study of race and culture; a Western critique of civil-society conditions is unavoidably bound up with them in the presupposition of a public discursive space in which the critique plays out. In some sense, *politics* has always meant contestation in the West, and an international model of culture will help keep this in focus (Chicago Cultural Studies Group). Both of these positions will confront us with the profoundly frustrating realization that hegemony as object of critique both resists criticism and makes it possible, and the corollary contingency that engaging in effective *intellectual* resistance of dominant-culture institutions may require a history of compliance with them.

And it is this awareness that may underscore West's desire for an unleashing of affect and emotion. To proscribe pathos as a dominant appeal in matters of race and culture is to discourage a sense of immediacy, to ignore the pain and suffering that accompanies injustice, to convert the corporeal to abstraction. Of course, a recognition of complicity in the very structures one hopes to change can lead to something like Victor's dilemma. We can wait for someone or something to carry us back where the footing is sure so that we may patrol the boundaries of our own understanding, or we can stand frozen, paralyzed by the likelihood that habituation will push back or absorb the unfamiliar as we move outward. The great value of *Signs of Struggle* is that West encourages us to make the most implicit of our ground rules explicit, not simply as an intellectual exercise, but to recognize the cost of not doing so.

*DePaul University*
*Chicago, Illinois*

# Notes

## Introduction

1. Sociologists Michael Omi and Howard Winant observe that the consolidation of various groups (and by association their differences) under a common signifier of race is a strategy in the move toward nationalism in racially hegemonic contexts such as the United States. Erasing differences in this manner enables the managing of the "raucous diversity" of "minority" positions: "Just as [colonial] conquest created the 'native' where once their had been Pequot, Iroquois, or Tutelo, so too it created the 'black' where once there had been Asante, Ovimbundu, Yoruba, or Bakongo" (Omi and Winant 66).

I use the terms "white" and "black" throughout this book as *signs of struggle,* indicating that they describe neither skin color nor biologically singular groups of people but contested socio-historical concepts stemming in part from the politics of race. Thus, bell hooks, for example, can speak of "postmodern blackness" as a form of identity politics wherein identity based on essentialism is critiqued while the connections among identity, politics, and shared experience are affirmed. The effects of the concepts of whiteness and blackness on cultural consciousness and subjectivity need to be addressed as we seek to move beyond them and examine the extraordinary diversity of subject positions, social experiences, and cultural identities that compose the categories.

Also, for more on "critical multiculturalism," see Giourx and McLaren, Gordon and Newfield, and particularly Goldberg.

127

## Chapter One

## Toward a Critical Theory of Negotiation and Hybridity

1. It is one thing to discuss theories of hybridity in terms of the individual, but a major challenge becomes how to conceive of group hybridity and exploit it *collectively*, toward social and political ends. In an interview with Lawrence Grossberg, Stuart Hall discusses Rastafarians in Jamaica as a coherent social and political group (re)formed by using cultural resources from the developing world in conjunction with language from the Bible for their own cultural and political purposes:

> In turning the text upside-down they remade themselves; they positioned themselves differently as new political subjects; they reconstructed themselves as blacks in the new world: they *became* what they are. And, positioning themselves in that way, they learned to speak a new language.... They did not assume that their only cultural resources lay in the past. They did not go back and try to recover some absolutely pure "folk culture," untouched by history, as if that would be the only way they could learn to speak. No, they made use of the modern media to broadcast their message.... This is cultural transformation. It is not something totally new. It is not something that has a straight, unbroken line of continuity from the past. It is transformation through a reorganization of the elements of a cultural practice, elements which do not in themselves have any necessary political connotations. It is not the individual elements of a discourse that have political or ideological connotations, it is the ways those elements are organized together in a new discursive formation. ("On Postmodernism" 143)

The point here is not to romanticize the Rastafarians but to see their efforts in this respect as a way to think of cultural processes of hybridity in collective terms.

Also, I do not want to be too uncritically celebratory about hybridity. Some postcolonial literature, such as Tayeb Salih's *Season of Migration to the North* and Tsitsi Dangarembga's *Nervous Conditions*, explores the troubling situation of people at the conflicted intersections of cultural hybridity. This position between cultures is "negotiated" in these novels with a great deal of difficulty and pain. In both of these novels, there are "hybrid" characters torn between the lure of European society and their own African heritages. In one case, the character attempts suicide and in the other becomes bulimic.

Anzaldúa also talks about the psychological effects of achieving a "border-land" or hybrid consciousness:

> In perceiving conflicting information and points of view, *la mestiza* is subjected to a swamping of her psychological borders. She has discovered that she can't hold concepts or ideas in rigid boundaries. The borders and walls that are supposed to keep the undesirable ideas out are entrenched habits and patterns of behavior; these habits and patterns are the enemy within. Rigidity means death. (79)

According to Anzaldúa, tolerance for ambiguity and contradiction is necessary for survival in borderland situations. And as Salih and Dangarembga explore, the effects of hybridity are often manifested at the level of the affective as well, taking toll on emotional and physical health. It is not because of the biological "fact" of hybridity that this affective tension occurs but because of the dominant, continuing influence of racial thinking that discourages thinking of hybridity in positive terms because it is seen as an "unnatural" state of being and, thus, inferior. The internalization of this kind of thinking about oneself is precisely what must be resisted, as Anzaldúa argues, and what can lead to such psychic and affective fallout as self-loathing, alienation, and shame. The point I am making here is that we cannot be too uncritically celebratory of hybridity because deep and pervasive structures of racial thinking continue to have real and formidable effects on those who need to achieve borderland or hybrid consciousness to survive.

2. As I will take up further in Chapters 4 and 5, it is important to better understand the operations of anger both in its insurgent and conservative capacities when discussing and studying the politics of cultural difference. Lyman also writes of the effect that rationality or civility has on how we perceive and receive anger and emotion:

> The rules of politeness and rationality that govern social dia-logues may make it impossible to say what needs to be said by making certain topics impolite, certain tones of voice or emo-tions irrational, or simply defining topics as psychological and not political. . . . A phenomenology of anger does not focus upon the means of expression of anger, but its *meaning*, the self-understanding and understanding of the world of the angry person. (59, 61)

When different groups meet and interact, anger sometimes surfaces, and it seems that a primary reflex is to think of ways of defusing that anger, of "negotiating" it. But such moves do not allow for us to learn how to hear what anger is being made to say, what anger is being asked to defend, how anger can act as a dialectic of self and world. We might think about how emotions such as anger influence the negotiation process, how negotiation is a process that seeks to defuse anger in the first place. Direct, angry speech poses challenges, yes, but anger is not something that always needs to be immediately defused. The challenge becomes how to listen critically, how to relate the political impulses of individual and collective anger to present and preceding social conditions.

Learning how to receive direct and critical speech, how not to take such criticism personally, to *think* it and not simply *feel* it is as important as learning how to craft critical arguments. Arguing for the need to *think* angry speech may seem at first glance contradictory. But what I am proposing is that we *(re)think* anger—in both its transgressive and conservative senses—in the processes of social, political, and pedagogical interaction, while we work to listen to the complicated dialectic between the social and the personal, a dialectic that often works on a deep affective level. Audre Lorde, for example, speaks of the anger that racism generates within her and says that one of the major tasks of her life was to learn *"how to train* that anger with accuracy rather than deny it" (145; emphasis added). We might think about how moral and political stances are articulated through anger and what implications these articulations have for pedagogical as well as social relations. Above all, listening to others as they express anger should not be turned into a form of placation: "I'm sorry you feel that way." In short, we might theorize the different ways that anger acts as an impetus for and as a hindrance to thoughtful social action. However, indifferent liberal conceptions of negotiation are inadequate to analyze and to critique the complicated rhetorical connections between the personal inflections and the political articulations of anger.

Also, Bhabha talks of the need to study anxiety as an effect of social transition and translation, and he thinks that anger, violence, and hatred are more than mere adjectives (angry, violent, hated) always attached to what is seen as something more substantial ("Staging" 34). Anger, violence, and hatred are themselves constitutive elements of the performative subject, in both individual and collective terms. That is, anger, violence, and hatred are more productively seen as components in the construction of group solidarity and identity. We might argue that hatred, for example, is key to the solidarity and affirmation of white supremacist groups, although many within these groups claim that cohesion depends on heritage.

## Chapter Two

## Rewriting the Difference of Race

1. It is interesting to note that ostensibly progressive television shows such as *Star Trek*, for example, also rely on such outmoded notions of race. Although

*Star Trek* is set in the future, it represents humans and aliens as races in the traditional sense—as separate categories of "people" with inherent behavioral traits and characteristics. For this reason, I sometimes use the show in cultural studies and rhetoric classes when discussing and interrogating concepts and representations of race. For an in-depth analysis of how race operates in *Star Trek*, including constructions of whiteness, see Daniel Leonard Bernardi's Star Trek *and History: Race-ing Toward a White Future.*

2. In order to complexify and nuance understandings of cultural identity and experience, some theorists have suggested thinking about cultural identities and subjectivities in terms of *ethnicity* rather than *race*. Stuart Hall, for example, writes, "The term ethnicity acknowledges the place of history, language and culture in the construction of subjectivity and identity, as well as the fact that all discourse is placed, positioned, situated, and all knowledge is contextual" (qtd. in Ashcroft et al. 226). There are important distinctions too between the concept of *race* and that of *ethnicity* as "ideologies of difference," distinctions that are couched in particular social and historical contexts. Whereas *race* is historically connected to slavery and colonialism, *ethnicity* is connected to issues of migration, immigration, and cultural contact, especially in the United States. How people have come to be "racialized" and "ethnicized," in many cases, describes a qualitatively different historical experience. In other words, race and ethnicity represent different politics of inscription or different ways of "othering" people because the concepts arise in different historical and social contexts, and their meanings are not interchangeable nor should they be confused or conflated.

Some important studies on race that I have found helpful include Tzvetan Todorov's *On Human Diversity*, Omi and Winant's *Racial Formation in the United States*, Goldberg's *Anatomy of Racism*, John Solomos and Les Back's *Racism and Society*, and Pieterse's *White on Black*. Angela Y. Davis' *Women, Race, and Class* and Glenda Elizabeth Gilmore's *Gender and Jim Crow* provide superb historical analyses of the interlocking structures of race and gender. Also, Edward Said's "An Ideology of Difference" (in Gates) and "Zionism from the Standpoint of Its Victims" (in Goldberg) are excellent studies of racism in non-Western contexts—in these cases, Israeli policy toward Palestine.

## Chapter Three

## Men's Studies, Feminism(s), and Rhetorics of Difference

1. See West, "The Racist Other."

2. I elaborate on the need for safe places in the face of discrimination and

violence in Chapter 5 when I talk about what I call "a praxis of shelter." In this sense, shelter acts as a space from which to develop alternative perspectives and as a place to regroup for resistance to those forces that generate the need for such shelter in the first place.

3. Micciche has critiqued Connors, arguing that by appealing to "paternalism, cultural standards, and patterns of masculine initiation, Connors contributes to Robert Bly's offensive against the debilitating effects of feminism" (23). Furthermore, she notes that in his article Connors collapses *feminisms* into one monologic *Feminism* (22). In much the same way, and equally troubling, he collapses *masculinities* into one (straight, white) *Masculinity*.

Although Connors has been critiqued by Micciche and others on these issues, he is responsible for helping to initiate dialogue in rhetorical theory on masculinity studies, something for which he should be commended and remembered.

4. I have heard people talk of the appropriation of the term "nigger" by some African-Americans as analogous to the appropriation of the term "queer" by many gays and lesbians. There certainly is a similar strategy at work of lessening the negative effects of the terms on identity formation, but there is an important difference as well. It seems that African-Americans generally are not arguing to reclaim the offensive and offending term. In other words, although the efforts of some African-Americans, particularly in the Blacks Arts Movement, have served to lessen the negative power of the term, it is not being thought of as a point from which to rally coherent political projects of positive self-reidentification to the extent of "queer."

## Chapter Four

### Rhetoric, Emotion, and the Affective Violence of Difference

1. As I will discuss more in the book's conclusion, Žižek also argues that we are entering a postpolitical age wherein the political is increasingly coming to be relegated to the negotiation of interests among technocrats, that the political is coming to be comprised of compromises reached in the guise of more or less universal consensus. In such a weakened political environment, violence, he goes on to say, can be seen as eruptions of the political, as seemingly politically incoherent expressions of dissatisfaction from those who feel that their interests are not being represented in the negotiation scheme ("Leftist," "Multiculturalism").

2. A good example of the kind of conservative politics of anger that I am

talking about can be seen in Spike Lee's *Jungle Fever*, a film I sometimes use in cultural studies courses. In it, the relationship between an African-American man and an Italian-American woman fails in part because of the tremendous pressure put on them by the anger of friends and family who cannot accept the "transgressive" nature of the relationship.

## Chapter Five

## From the Safe House to a Praxis of Shelter

1. Uncomplicated understandings of experience take it that one's experiences validate claims to cultural identity and vice versa. Joan Scott writes that in much current usage of experience, "references to structure and history are implied but never made explicit; instead, personal testimony of oppression replaces analysis and explanation and comes to stand for the experience of the group" (219–20). She warns against the reduction of experience to an idea of unmediated, direct access to the truth. Also, in "Reading and Writing Differences: The Problematic of Experience," Min-Zhan Lu argues for teaching an understanding of experience as "experiential" *and* analytical, one that problematizes the "authority" of experience.

It is a major premise of this book that critical projects and politics are not just about speaking from and for one's own experiences and physio-cultural positioning—although these connections are obviously fundamental—but from positioning based on commitments, principles, politics, and theory as well. Although not a new idea, such crossover work, as it has been called, continually requires critical negotiation and imagination wherein identity politics based on essentialism are critiqued while the connections between identity and politics is affirmed. I think that such connecting itself can lead to new identities, hybrid and perhaps provisional ones, transculturally constituted nonetheless from preceding social conditions.

2. A similar point about the frustration felt by those who are repeatedly discouraged from speaking was recently made to me by a colleague who teaches women's studies courses. In the introductory women's studies classes that she teaches, male students sometimes begin to argue straight away with feminist positions and stances being articulated and discussed. My colleague recalls one male student asking in a moment of desperation after much retaliation to his interrupting, "Well, what do you women want?" To which she replied, "We just want you to shut up for a while and listen."

3. *Marronage* is a good example of a kind of active sheltering work that I am talking about. Michael Omi and Howard Winant write, "*Marronage* refers to the practice, widespread throughout the Americas, whereby runaway slaves

formed communities in remote areas such as swamps, mountains, or forests, often in alliance with dispossessed indigenous peoples" (185). The Seminoles of Florida, for example, began as a collection of escaped slaves and indigenous Florida tribes displaced by the Spanish. Later, Cherokees displaced from Georgia, South Carolina, and Alabama by white plantation owners and federal troops joined with these others. These various groups ended up collecting in the swamps and salt marsh flats of the south Florida everglades, where they staged a series of successful battles with federal troops led by Andrew Jackson, Oglethorpe, and others. Relatively few Seminoles remain, however, most being either killed or forced to move West. Still, *marronage* offers a helpful model for a praxis of shelter, a place created for protection from oppression and a place from which both to stage collective resistance to that oppression and to form alternative perspectives. In the case of escaped slaves, resistance was connected to education and to the acquisition of literacy, as well as to the planning of marauding expeditions and uprisings.

Of course, *marronage* is only a theoretical guideline for a praxis of shelter. Pedagogical and social forums present challenges that I think can be met by better understanding the political and rhetorical dimensions of anger and by using strategies of perseverance, patience, and listening in ways that set the groundwork for productive ideological conflict rather than undercut it.

## (Against) Conclusion

## Taking It Outside, or, Rhetoric and Politics Beyond the Pale

1. I said in Chapter 2 that Mouffe's distinctions between agonism and antagonism and between adversary and enemy was useful in distinguishing between a politics of anger and a politics of hate. That being said, however, I find her definition of "enemy" troublesome. Mouffe defines "enemies" in *The Return of the Political* as those who "do not accept the democratic 'rules of the game' and who thereby exclude themselves from the political community" (4). A definition of enemies as those who "do not accept the democratic 'rules of the game' and who thereby exclude themselves from the political community" is problematic and, to me, not particularly radical because it encourages seeing extreme "politics" as non-political. Such a definition of enemy goes against what I am arguing for in this chapter: 1) the need to stress and disrupt if necessary restrictive rules and criteria of political community, and 2) the need to realize that the "rules of the game" are largely drawn up by those with the power to institute their ways with language in order to exclude positions and locate them outside the realm of the political. Of course, there are those groups that choose to opt out of the game—anti-federal government paramilitary extremists, for example. (And I still would not call them non-political.) But there are many

others who find themselves outside and excluded not by their own choosing but by the very politics of othering that I have been critiquing all along. Although Mouffe is clearly working against a conception of politics that is rationalist, I find the "rules-of-the-game" part of her definition of enemy troublesome. It is clear to me that any politics of exclusion and the ways in which positions become relegated to the non-political should be at issue.

Donna Strickland argues that radical democratic agendas need to deploy the discourse and ideals of democracy so as to question all aspects of what currently passes for "democratic" society. She suggests that we "worry" democracy "by demonstrating the ways in which forms of exclusion and subordination continue to function" in "democratic" contexts (481, 483).

Also, for more on radical democracy, see Trend.

2. We might also consider how "minority" positions do not act in any significant way, according to dominant positions, on the composition of culture in overtly repressive situations. In this respect, James C. Scott's *Weapons of the Weak: Everyday Forms of Peasant Resistance* and *Domination and the Arts of Resistance: Hidden Transcripts* are illustrative. Describing his anthropological work in small farming villages of Malay, Scott posits "unofficial transcripts" as those forms of resistance, affirmation, and identification—those unauthorized scripts for acting—that occur "off stage," outside of "official transcripts," or out of sight of capricious landlords and masters. Such covert resistance occurs in contexts in which open and outright resistance would be met with brutal countermeasures or public humiliation. Pilfering, poaching, and sabotage are considered forms of insubordination we might call the infrapolitics or micropolitics of the powerless (*Domination* xiii). Part of Scott's objective is to "suggest how we might successfully read, interpret, and understand the often fugitive political conduct of subordinate groups" and to make a case for "a different study of power, that uncovers contradictions, tensions, and immanent possibilities" (xii).

# Works Cited

Alcoff, Linda Martín. "The Problem of Speaking for Others." *Who Can Speak: Authority and Critical Identity*. Ed. Judith Roof and Robyn Wiegman. Urbana: U of Illinois P, 1995. 97–119.

———. "What Should White People Do?" *Hypatia: A Journal of Feminist Philosophy* 13.3 (1998): 6–26.

Anzaldúa, Gloria. *Borderlands/La Frontera: The New Mestiza*. San Francisco: Aunt Lute, 1987.

Ashton-Jones, Evelyn. "Collaboration, Conversation, and the Politics of Gender." *Feminine Principles and Women's Experience in American Composition and Rhetoric*. Ed. Louise Phelps and Janet Emig. Pittsburgh: U of Pittsburgh P, 1995. 5–26.

Bartky, Sandra Lee. *Femininity and Domination: Studies in the Phenomenology of Oppression*. New York: Routledge, 1990.

———. "Foreword." *Men Doing Feminism*. Ed. Tom Digby. New York: Routledge, 1998. xi–xiv.

Berlant, Lauren, and Michael Warner. "Introduction to 'Critical Multiculturalism.'" Goldberg. 107–13.

Berlin, James. *Rhetorics, Poetics, and Cultures: Refiguring College English Studies*. Urbana: NCTE, 1996.

137

Bhabha, Homi K. "Are You a Man or a Mouse?" *Constructing Masculinity*. Ed. Maurice Berger, Brian Wallis, and Simon Watson. New York: Routledge, 1995. 57–65.

———. "Culture's In-Between." *Questions of Cultural Identity*. Ed. Stuart Hall and Paul du Gay. London: Sage, 1996. 53–60.

———. *The Location of Culture*. London: Routledge, 1994.

———. "Staging the Politics of Difference: Homi Bhabha's Critical Literacy." Interview with Gary A. Olson and Lynn Worsham. *Race, Rhetoric, and the Postcolonial*. Ed. Gary A. Olson and Lynn Worsham. Albany: State U of New York P, 1999. 3–39.

Bizzell, Patricia. "'Contact Zones' and English Studies." *College English* 56 (1994): 163–69.

Bizzell, Patricia, and Bruce Herzberg, eds. *Negotiating Difference: Cultural Case Studies for Composition*. Boston: St. Martin's, 1996.

Brod, Harry. "The Case for Men's Studies." *The Making of Masculinities: The New Men's Studies*. Ed. Harry Brod. Boston: Allen and Unwin, 1987. 39–62.

Brod, Harry, and Michael Kaufman, eds. *Theorizing Masculinities*. Thousand Oaks, CA: Sage, 1994.

Brodkey, Linda. *Writing Permitted in Designated Areas Only*. Minneapolis: U of Minnesota P, 1996.

Butler, Judith. "Contingent Foundations." *Feminists Theorize the Political*. Ed. Judith Butler and Joan W. Scott. New York: Routledge, 1992. 3–21.

———. *Gender Trouble: Feminism and the Subversion of Identity*. New York: Routledge, 1990.

Caldwell, Mark. *A Short History of Rudeness: Manners, Morals, and Misbehavior in Modern America*. New York: St. Martin's, 1999.

Canagarajah, A. Suresh. "Safe Houses in the Contact Zone: Coping Strategies of African-American Students in the Academy." *College Composition and Communication* 48 (1997): 173–96.

Chambers, Iain. "Signs of Silence, Lines of Listening." *The Post-Colonial*

*Question: Common Skies, Divided Horizons.* Ed. Iain Chambers and Lidia Curti. London: Routledge, 1996. 47–62.

Clinton, Catherine. "Contents Under Pressure: White Woman/Black History." *Skin Deep: Black Women and White Women Write about Race.* Ed. Marita Golden and Susan Richards Shreve. New York: Anchor, 1996. 238–55.

Cloud, Dana L. *Control and Consolation in American Culture and Politics: Rhetorics of Therapy.* Thousand Oaks, CA: Sage, 1998.

Connell, R.W. "Politics of Changing Men." *Socialist Review* 25.1 (1995): 135–59.

Connors, Robert J. "Teaching and Learning as a Man." *College English* 58 (1996): 137–57.

Culler, Jonathan. "Five Propositions on the Future of Men in Feminism." *Men Writing the Feminine: Literature, Theory, and the Questions of Gender.* Ed. Thaïs E. Morgan. Albany: State U of New York P, 1994. 187–88.

Dangarembga, Tsitsi. *Nervous Conditions.* Seattle: Seal, 1989.

Dyer, Richard. "White." *Screen* 29.4 (1988): 44–64.

———. *White.* London: Routledge, 1997.

Dyson, Michael Eric. "Race and the Public Intellectual: A Conversation with Michael Eric Dyson." Interview with Sidney I. Dobrin. *JAC: A Journal of Composition Theory* 17 (1997): 143–81.

Ebert, Teresa L. "The 'Difference' of Postmodern Feminism." *College English* 53 (1991): 886–904.

Fanon, Frantz. *The Wretched of the Earth.* Trans. Constance Farrington. New York: Grove, 1963.

Fish, Stanley. *There's No Such Thing as Free Speech, and It's a Good Thing Too.* Oxford: Oxford UP, 1994.

Fox, Robert Elliot. "Becoming Post-White." *MultiAmerica: Essays on Cultural Wars and Cultural Peace.* Ed. Ishmael Reed. New York: Viking, 1997. 6–17.

Frankenberg, Ruth, ed. *Displacing Whiteness: Essays in Social and Cultural Criticism.* Durham: Duke UP, 1997.

————. *White Women, Race Matters: The Social Construction of Whiteness.* Minneapolis: U of Minnesota P, 1993.

Fraser, Nancy. *Justice Interruptus: Critical Reflections on the "Postsocialist" Condition.* New York: Routledge, 1997.

Fuss, Diana. *Essentially Speaking: Feminism, Nature, and Difference.* New York: Routledge, 1989.

Garvey, John, and Noel Ignatiev. "Toward a New Abolitionism: A *Race Traitor* Manifesto." Hill 346–49.

Gates, Henry Louis, Jr., ed. *"Race," Writing, and Difference.* Chicago: U of Chicago P, 1986.

Giroux, Henry A. *Border Crossings: Cultural Workers and the Politics of Education.* New York: Routledge, 1992.

————. "Racial Politics and the Pedagogy of Whiteness." Hill. 294–315.

Giroux, Henry A., and Peter McLaren. *Between Borders: Pedagogy and the Politics of Cultural Studies.* New York: Routledge, 1994.

Goldberg, David Theo, ed. *Multiculturalism: A Critical Reader.* Oxford: Blackwell, 1994.

Gordon, Avery F., and Christopher Newfield, eds. *Mapping Multiculturalism.* Minneapolis: U of Minnesota P, 1996.

Gossett, Thomas F. *Race: The History of an Idea in America.* 2nd ed. New York: Oxford UP, 1997.

Greenbaum, Andrea. "'Wat'cha Think? I Can't Spell?': Constructing Literacy in the Postcolonial Classroom." *Composition Forum* 9 (1998): 1–9.

Grosz, Elizabeth. "Sexual Difference and the Problem of Essentialism." *The Essential Difference.* Ed. Naomi Schor and Elizabeth Weed. Bloomington: Indiana UP, 1994. 82–97.

Hall, Stuart. "Cultural Composition: Stuart Hall on Ethnicity and the Discursive Turn." Interview with Julie Drew. *JAC: A Journal of Composition Theory* 18 (1998). 171–96.

————. "New Ethnicities." *The Post-Colonial Studies Reader.* Ed. Bill Ashcroft,

Gareth Griffiths, and Helen Tiffin. London: Routledge, 1995. 223–27.

———. "On Postmodernism and Articulation: An Interview with Stuart Hall." Interview with Lawrence Grossberg. *Stuart Hall: Critical Dialogues in Cultural Studies*. Ed. David Morley and Kuan-Hsing Chen. London: Routledge, 1996. 131–50.

Haraway, Donna. "Writing, Literacy, and Technology: Toward a Cyborg Writing." Interview with Gary A. Olson. *JAC: A Journal of Composition Theory* 16 (1996): 1–26.

Harding, Sandra. "Starting from Marginalized Lives: A Conversation with Sandra Harding." Interview with Elizabeth Hirsh and Gary A. Olson. *JAC: A Journal of Composition Theory* 15 (1995): 193–225.

Harris, Joseph. *A Teaching Subject: Composition Since 1966*. Upper Saddle River, NJ: Prentice, 1997.

Hearn, Jeff, and David L. Collinson. "Theorizing Unities and Differences Between Men and Between Masculinities." Brod and Kaufman. 97–118.

Heath, Stephen. "Male Feminism." Jardine and Smith. 1–32.

Hill, Mike, ed. *Whiteness: A Critical Reader*. New York: New York UP, 1997.

hooks, bell. *Feminist Theory: From Margin to Center*. Boston: South End, 1984.

———. *Sisters of the Yam: Black Women and Self-Recovery*. Boston: South End, 1993.

———. *Teaching to Transgress: Education as the Practice of Freedom*. New York: Routledge, 1994.

———. *Yearning: Race, Gender, and Cultural Politics*. Boston: South End, 1990.

Hurd, Denise Alessandria. "The Monster Inside: 19th Century Racial Constructs in the 24th Century Mythos of *Star Trek*." *Journal of Popular Culture* 31 (1997): 23–35.

Ignatiev, Noel, and John Garvey, eds. *Race Traitor*. New York: Routledge, 1996.

Jameson, Fredric. "On 'Cultural Studies.'" *Social Text* 34 (1993): 17–52.

Jardine, Alice, and Paul Smith, eds. *Men in Feminism*. New York: Routledge, 1987.

Jarratt, Susan C. "Feminism and Composition: The Case for Conflict." *Contending with Words: Composition and Rhetoric in a Postmodern Age*. Ed. Patricia Harkin and John Schilb. New York: MLA, 1991. 105–23.

Keating, AnnLouise. "Interrogating 'Whiteness,' (De)Constructing 'Race.'" *College English* 57 (1995): 901–18.

Kimmel, Michael S. "Masculinity as Homophobia: Fear, Shame, and Silence in the Construction of Gender Identity." Brod and Kaufman. 119–41.

Kimmel, Michael S., and Michael A. Messner, eds. *Men's Lives*. 4th ed. Boston: Allyn, 1998.

Kingwell, Mark. *A Civil Tongue: Justice, Dialogue, and the Politics of Pluralism*. University Park, PA: Pennsylvania State UP, 1995.

LaCapra, Dominick, ed. *The Bounds of Race: Perspectives on Hegemony and Resistance*. Ithaca: Cornell UP, 1991.

Lorde, Audre. *Sister Outsider: Essays and Speeches by Audre Lorde*. Freedom, CA: Crossing P, 1996.

Lu, Min-Zhan. "Conflict and Struggle: The Enemies or Preconditions of Basic Writing?" *College English* 54 (1992): 887–913.

———. "Reading and Writing Differences: The Problematic of Experience." *Feminism and Composition Studies: In Other Words*. Ed. Susan C. Jarratt and Lynn Worsham. New York: MLA, 1998. 239–51.

Lyman, Peter. "The Politics of Anger: On Silence, Ressentiment, and Political Speech." *Socialist Review* 11.3 (1981): 55–74.

MacKinnon, Catharine A. *Only Words*. Cambridge: Harvard UP, 1996.

Mahala, Daniel, and Jody Swilky. "Constructing the Multicultural Subject: Colonization, Persuasion, and Difference in the Writing Classroom." *PRE/TEXT* 15 (1994): 182–216.

Marcuse, Herbert. "Repressive Tolerance." *A Critique of Pure Tolerance*. Robert Paul Wolff, Barrington Moore, Jr., and Herbert Marcuse. Boston: Beacon, 1965. 81–123.

Martin, April. "Fruits, Nuts, and Chocolate: The Politics of Sexual Identity." *The Harvard Gay and Lesbian Review*. Ed. Richard Schneider. Philadelphia: Temple UP, 1997. 322–33.

Martin, Biddy. "Sexualities Without Gender and Other Queer Utopias." *Diacritics* 24.2–3 (1994): 104–21.

May, Larry. *Masculinity and Morality*. Ithaca: Cornell UP, 1998.

May, Larry, Robert Strikwerda, and Patrick D. Hopkins. *Rethinking Masculinity: Philosophical Explorations in the Light of Feminism*. 2nd ed. Lanham, MD: Rowman, 1996.

Mercer, Kobena. "Skin Head Sex Thing: Racial Difference and the Homoerotic Imaginary." *How Do I Look? Queer Film and Video*. Ed. Bad Object-Choices. Seattle: Bay P, 1991. 169–210.

Messner, Michael A. *Politics of Masculinities: Men in Movements*. Thousand Oaks, CA: Sage, 1997.

Micciche, Laura R. "Male Plight and Feminist Threat to Composition Studies: A Response to 'Teaching and Learning as a Man.'" *Composition Studies* 25 (1997): 21–36.

Mohanty, Chandra Talpade. "On Race and Voice: Challenges for Liberal Education in the 1990s." Giroux and McLaren. 145–66.

Mouffe, Chantal. "Rethinking Political Community: Chantal Mouffe's Liberal Socialism." Interview with Lynn Worsham and Gary A. Olson. *JAC: A Journal of Composition Theory* 19 (1999): 163–99.

———. *The Return of the Political*. New York: Verso, 1993.

Nehring, Neil. *Popular Music, Gender, and Postmodernism: Anger Is an Energy*. Thousand Oaks, CA: Sage, 1997.

Olds, Sharon. *The Gold Cell*. New York: Knopf, 1992.

Olson, Gary A. "Encountering the Other: Postcolonial Theory and Composition Scholarship." *JAC: A Journal of Composition Theory* 18 (1998): 45–55.

Omi, Michael, and Howard Winant. *Racial Formation in the United States: From the 1960s to the 1990s*. 2nd ed. New York: Routledge, 1994.

Pieterse, Jan Nederveen. *White on Black: Images of Africa and Blacks in Popular Culture*. New Haven: Yale UP, 1992.

Pratt, Mary Louise. "Arts of the Contact Zone." *Profession 91* (1991): 33–40.

Putnam, Robert D. "Bowling Alone: America's Declining Social Capital." *Journal of Democracy* 6.1 (1995): 65–78.

Read, Daphnae. "Writing Trauma, History, Story: The Class(room) as Borderland." *JAC: A Journal of Composition Theory* 18 (1998): 105–21.

Real, Terrence. *I Don't Want to Talk about It: Overcoming the Secret Legacy of Male Depression*. New York: Fireside, 1998.

Rich, Adrienne. *Blood, Bread, and Poetry: Selected Prose 1979–1985*. New York: Norton, 1994.

Roman, Leslie G. "White Is a Color! White Defensiveness, Postmodernism, and Anti-racist Pedagogy." *Race, Identity, and Representation in Education*. New York: Routledge, 1993. 71–88.

Russo, Ann. "'We Cannot Live Without Our Lives': White Women, Antiracism, and Feminism." *Third World Women and the Politics of Feminism*. Ed. Chandra Talpade Mohanty, Ann Russo, and Lourdes Torres. Bloomington: Indiana UP, 1991. 297–313.

Said, Edward. Gates. "An Ideology of Difference." 38–58.

Salih, Tayeb. *Season of Migration to the North*. Trans. Denys Johnson-Davies. Portsmouth: Heinemann, 1995.

Scott, James C. *Domination and the Arts of Resistance: Hidden Transcripts*. New Haven: Yale UP, 1990.

Scott, Joan Wallach. "Campus Communities Beyond Consensus." *Beyond PC: Towards a Politics of Understanding*. Ed. Patricia Aufderheide. St. Paul, MN: Graywolf P, 1992. 213–24.

Sedgwick, Eve Kosofsky. "Gosh, Boy George, You Must Be Awfully Secure in Your Masculinity." *Constructing Masculinity*. Ed. Maurice Berger, Brian Wallis, and Simon Watson. New York: Routledge, 1995. 11–20.

Sheffield, Carol J. "Sexual Terrorism." *Women: A Feminist Perspective*. 4th ed. Ed. Jo Freeman. Mountain View, CA: Mayfield, 1989. 3–19.

Solomos, John, and Les Back. *Racism and Society*. New York: St. Martin's, 1996.

Strickland, Donna. "Worrying Democracy: Chantal Mouffe and the Return of Politicized Rhetoric." *JAC: A Journal of Composition Theory* 19 (1999): 476–83.

Tobin, Lad. "Car Wrecks, Baseball Caps, and Man-to-Man Defense: The Personal Narratives of Adolescent Males." *College English* 58 (1996): 158–75.

Trend, David, ed. *Radical Democracy: Identity, Citizenship, and the State*. New York: Routledge, 1996.

Trimbur, John. "Consensus and Difference in Collaborative Learning." *College English* 51 (1989): 602–16.

"An Unwise Road in Texas." Editorial. *The Economist* 20–26 June 1998: 17.

West, Cornel. *Keeping Faith: Philosophy and Race in America*. New York: Routledge, 1994.

West, Thomas. "Beyond Dissensus: Exploring the Heuristic Value of Conflict." *Rhetoric Review* 15 (1996): 142–55.

———. "The Racist Other." *JAC: A Journal of Composition Theory* 17 (1997): 215–26.

Williams, Raymond. *Problems in Materialism and Culture: Selected Essays*. London: Verso, 1980.

Winant, Howard. *Racial Conditions: Politics, Theories, Comparisons*. Minneapolis: U of Minnesota P, 1994.

Worsham, Lynn. "Going Postal: Pedagogic Violence and the Schooling of Emotion." *JAC: A Journal of Composition Theory* 18 (1998): 213–245.

———. "Romancing the Stones: My Movie Date with Sandra Harding." *JAC: A Journal of Composition Theory* 15 (1995): 565–71.

Young, Iris Marion. *Justice and the Politics of Difference*. Princeton: Princeton UP, 1990.

Young, Robert J.C. *Colonial Desire: Hybridity in Theory, Culture, and Race.* London: Routledge, 1995.

Žižek, Slavoj. "A Leftist Plea for 'Eurocentrism.'" *Critical Inquiry* 24 (1998): 988–1009.

———. "Multiculturalism, or, the Logic of Multinational Capitalism." *New Left Review* 225 (1997): 28–51.

# Index